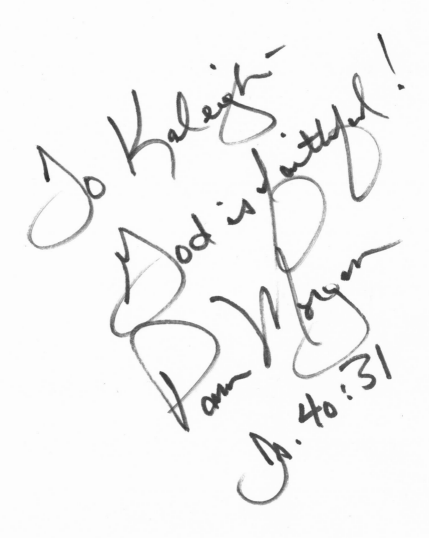

To Kaleigh-
God is faithful!

Pam Morgan

Is. 40:31

I STAND

I STAND

PAM MORGAN
AND BRENDA BLACK

JUBALEE PRESS

Published by Jubalee Press
P. O. Box 1991, Lee's Summit, MO 64063

Cover photo: Dan Laurine, The Loft Photography
Design and layout: Phil Morgan

First Printing: July 2009
Printed in the United States of America
10 9 8 7 6 5 4 3

ISBN 978-0-578-02781-4

To learn more about Pam Morgan and her ministry, visit her website:
www.WalkingMiracle.com

To Phil, Kayla, and Alisha:

You are my world – the source of my deepest happiness.

To my Jesus:

You are my everything – the source of my deepest joy.

Contents

A Note from Pam

If you are recovering from a recent life-changing tragedy, and someone gave you this book to "help you feel better" or to "help you find joy or God's purpose in the pain," you have my sympathy. Many additions to my own library were gifts intended to do the same – to "fix" my pain.

I began reading one such book out of deep respect for the giver, yet I slammed it shut several pages past the cover, disgusted that the author had the audacity to suggest joy was always a choice. Much to my surprise, several years later I picked up that same book only to find the author had incredible insight. I understood every word like it was my own. I couldn't put the book down.

When I initially started reading it, my heart, mind and soul were clouded in grief. And that was okay. *"There is a time for everything, and a season for every activity under heaven." -* Eccl. 3:1. There is a season to mourn. Scripture confirms it.

If you are in that season right now, life stinks. I know. Been there, done that. But as you are able...keep reading. You don't have to read the whole thing now. Just don't give up. Even though it may not seem like it, there *is* hope.

As you will see, my memories from the first two weeks after the accident are spotty at best. I pieced the days together from interviews with family, friends, doctors, EMTs, and even others at the scene who have kept in touch. I dissected medical records and received input from compassionate passers-by that stopped to help. The story is told as accurately as possible. Specific dialogue may not be quoted verbatim, but the conversations are real. I am not a mind reader, so thoughts of others are included only as they were disclosed during my research interviews.

With all the pieces in place, my story clearly reveals God's deep and multi-faceted truth. Each time I think about what has happened, I see another reflection of my Lord – another direct and profound application of scripture – and my faith continues to grow. All for another book perhaps.

For now, my grief has turned to rejoicing – yes, to joy. Years have passed, and I marvel at God's love, provision, and purpose in my life. This isn't just my story, it's God's story. I never tire of recounting it. I guess that's just how it is with broken vessels. Once God puts them back together and pours life into them, His "living water" continuously flows through the cracks. I praise my Savior for that! And I praise Him that He can put you back together as well and fill you with living water sweeter than you've ever tasted. All you have to do is ask. Now turn the page. Draw near, and drink.

Pam Morgan

I STAND

Famous Last Words

...don't take a single day for granted.
Take delight in each light-filled hour...
ECCLESIASTES 11:8

June 4, 2000 -

"91/94, you have a stat run MVA. Your time is 15:51."

Radio static crackled behind the dispatcher's urgent voice.

The paramedic grabbed his gear and hurried toward the ambulance at Bates County Memorial Hospital in Butler, Missouri. Bursting through the bay doors, he slid into the passenger seat on a balmy June Sunday where his EMT partner already waited with the motor running. Sirens blared as they pulled away. He recorded the time – 3:53 p.m. – and turned up the volume on the VHF radio scanner hoping to hear more detail from the Sheriff's office.

"There's a 1050 on the Miami Creek Bridge, a J-2, possibly a J-4."

They knew the codes well – injury accident, possibly a fatality. Pressing calls were the nature of their job. They knew there was no time to waste. Speeding down southbound Highway 71 toward

13

the Miami Creek Bridge, every minute counted. Delays could mean the difference between life and death.

As they neared the bridge, traffic slowed and surrendered to the emergency entourage. Suddenly a white van, flipped on its side, popped into view. Behind it, a battered, roofless utility trailer slumped on 3 wheels. At 3:58 they pulled beside the wreckage and jumped out. A state trooper pointed toward a bloody heap against the concrete barrier.

"Your fatality is over there on the bridge," he directed.

The experienced paramedic didn't doubt the trooper's words as he neared the body. Obviously thrown from the vehicle at high speed, this woman most likely died on impact. He quickly brushed the bystanders aside and knelt down beside her. In all his years of service, he never saw anyone survive injuries as severe as these, but touching the woman's shoulder, he was taken by surprise.

"Please God, help me..." she gasped.

———◦◦◦———

I don't remember my desperate plea for help that day. All I recall is the peace I felt in the hours beforehand. In the prime of my life, I never could have predicted how everything would change in a brief second.

My husband woke me that morning after only four hours of sleep. Rising before the sun wasn't unusual on weekends. Our concert schedule typically required it. But the outdoor music festival we hosted the day before ran later than expected, and we were pooped. Nevertheless, we had to get moving as this morning's concert was two hours down the road. So we piled our sleeping daughters, Kayla – five years old, and Alisha – twenty-one months, into the van. Grass glistened with heavy dew, and birds chirped cheerful good-mornings, eager to meet the day. We, on the other hand, were too tired to return the greeting.

Exiting our subdivision, we prayed, "Lord, thank you for yet another opportunity to serve you today. Guard and protect us as we travel..." A couple of hours later we pulled into the drive of

Merwin Christian Church. Reverend Alan Black, our good friend, greeted us in the parking lot. Four years ago, we held our first concert here. How ironic that we would return where we began on this day.

Alan and his wife, Brenda, are among our closest friends and join us in an accountability group of five couples we fondly dubbed "RELIEF." No relation to the familiar antacid commercial exists, although the guys readily joke about it. We girls roll our eyes and pretend not to find our husbands' fifth grade humor all that funny. After all, it's a woman's duty to at least appear sophisticated and refined. But no, the name is actually an acronym for Ready Encouragement Lies in Excellent Friends. We have grown so comfortable with one another, we can joke like children, laughing until it hurts, and still challenge each other with deep, spiritual truths. In today's world, such relationships are indeed a relief.

Most of our accountability group joined us for worship and lunch. After all, few could pass up Brenda's home-cooked lasagna. The morning and afternoon passed all too quickly in the company of good friends, and before our hearts were ready to leave, the clock reminded us our day was not done. Another concert in Stockton still lay ahead that evening, another hour and a half down the road. At three o'clock that afternoon we headed for our Ford Econoline once again. I strapped Alisha, sweaty, tired, and cranky into her car seat. Phil started the engine and turned the A/C on high.

"Would you like us to take the girls?" Allyson asked as I hugged her goodbye. "You can pick them up on your way home. It's on the way."

Dave and Allyson live on 40 acres with their two boys, who are the same ages as Kayla and Alisha. They raise horses, cows, cats, and at the time Colin, an old yellow lab who just wanted to nap and be loved. The girls would feel at home there and find lots to do, but my maternal instinct kicked in. Kayla and Alisha were exhausted and showed it. They were often hard to handle when fighting sleep.

"No, thanks," I said hesitantly. "We'd better take them with us."

I turned to find Alisha already sound asleep, confirming my decision. I didn't want to wake her now. A decent nap was exactly what she needed, and with the car seat straps snug against her chest, I could rest easily, confident of my daughter's safety. My little "Houdini" hated confinement. Usually she maneuvered herself free of the car seat straps behind my back during the ride. Relieved, I shifted focus to my eldest daughter, still wide awake.

"Kayla, do you want me to sit in the back with you, until you fall asleep?"

Kayla nodded and bounded onto the back sofa seat.

"Babe, you drive…I'll fall asleep if I do."

Phil agreed upon my promise to crawl up to the front passenger seat once Kayla fell asleep. Exhausted himself, I knew he needed help staying alert.

I climbed in behind Kayla, frustrated to see that all except the center seat belt had fallen through the cushions. I didn't feel like twisting myself into a pretzel on the floor to retrieve them. *Oh well*, I thought and sighed. *I'll only be here for a few minutes.*

I strapped the lap belt around Kayla and pulled it snug to her hips. Then sinking into the soft sofa seat to her right, I waved goodbye to our friends still standing in the gravel drive.

"Rock and roll!" Jamie Jones shouted with a twinkle in his eye.

They waved and turned toward the house as we embarked onto the two-lane blacktop. I leaned my head back against the headrest; letting the cool breeze flow over me from the vents overhead.

This feels so good, I thought, *I'll close my eyes just for a minute.*

Fifteen minutes later Phil glanced into the rear view mirror as he merged southbound on 71 Highway. I was limp with sleep. Kayla rested peacefully against my shoulder and her eyes bobbed heavily to a close. All was quiet.

So much for conversation to keep me awake, Phil thought. He accelerated to 70 miles per hour and switched to the smoother ride of the left lane, setting the cruise control. The radio was out of the question – too much noise for his resting family. Phil turned the A/C thermostat to the coldest setting.

There…frigid air should help…I can make it.

About six miles south of Butler, Phil glanced at the clock – 3:51 p.m. – right on schedule. He yawned. The steady drone of tires on the pavement was tranquilizing. Phil tried reading road signs, billboards…anything to stay awake. Approaching the Miami Creek Bridge on the right, a large red cardinal painted on the side of a vacant semi trailer advertised a local tree farm.

Phil blinked, struggling to resist his heavy eyelids. He blinked again. And again, slower this time. His eyes lingered shut a few seconds longer. Forcing them open, he flinched to see the guardrail looming directly ahead. Quickly he jerked the wheel back toward the narrow highway. It was too late. The front left tire ascended the metal rail and flew off as it slammed back to the ground. The speed and force of the hit was so extreme, the van toppled over on its side. Phil's window shattered; screeching concrete raced beside his ear until the van slid to a stop across the two lane bridge. The bumper barely kissed the creek's concrete barrier, the only thing that kept it from dropping into the rushing water below.

In an instant, all was deathly quiet except for the sound of Phil's heartbeat throbbing in his ears. Unbuckling his seatbelt, Phil placed his feet where the driver's window had been and stood on shaky legs. Alisha's car seat lay face down behind him. Still strapped inside, his baby girl was now wide awake and afraid. She started to cry. Phil set her upright and carefully made his way to the back sofa where Kayla hung from her lap belt.

"Where's Mommy?" Phil asked, anxiously releasing his other whimpering daughter and holding her close. I was missing, and the rear left window, now against the ground, was gone.

"I don't know," Kayla cried.

"Watch your sister while I go and find Mommy," he said.

Phil set Kayla down and reached for the doors overhead. Pain stabbed his shoulder, but he ignored it. He had to get out. Gravity pushed the heavy doors closed again and again until rushing adrenaline finally fueled him to fling them open. Phil forced his six-foot-one-inch, 250 pound frame up through the escape hatch, swung his feet over the side, and jumped to the ground.

A young man was already there, eager to help.

"My daughters are still in there," Phil said, "but I need to find my wife."

"She's behind the trailer," he said. "My wife knows CPR and is with her. Go, I'll get the girls out."

"I'll be right back," Phil called to Kayla and Alisha, trying to comfort.

Phil found the young woman leaning over my crumpled body against the concrete barrier of the bridge. She and her husband watched the whole accident in horror from the car behind us. Instinctively they pulled over. At the sound of crying children, he rushed to the van. She hurried to my side, prepared to perform CPR, but stopped herself. Although I wasn't breathing, she knew the slightest movement could be disastrous with injuries so excessive. Only one option remained. Dropping to her knees, she prayed.

"These babies need their mommy, Lord!" she begged, hearing our daughter's young, fearful cries.

Within seconds, I coughed and started to cry.

"Don't move," the young woman said.

A Missouri State Trooper spotted the wreckage on routine highway patrol when cars ahead suddenly veered onto the shoulder. Immediately he summoned emergency assistance and pulled over to divert traffic. As he jumped out of his patrol car, another woman darted across the divided highway.

"I'm a nurse," she said.

The trooper tossed her his medical kit.

A pool of blood surrounded me and rippled over the asphalt into a nearby drain. The two women knelt beside me as Phil paced between me and the van.

"Forgive me, Lord, I fell asleep," he confessed, torn by which direction to go – toward his wife or back to his daughters?

"Get down here and pray with us," the nurse said, overhearing.

"Is she alive?" he said.

"Yes, she's breathing."

Phil made his way through a maze of scattered speakers and broken glass and got down on his knees. He watched as I gasped for air with each breath. At the sound of our terrified daughters, Phil quickly realized he could do nothing more for me. They, on the other hand, needed him desperately. Safe in the care of a grandparent-like couple who supplied cookies and band-aids, Kayla and Alisha yearned for Daddy's familiar arms.

"God, this is out of my hands," he surrendered. "You've got to take care of Pam now."

As soon as he retreated, a woman stopped and introduced herself as a respiratory therapist. Immediately following her, a man approached, explaining he was an anesthesiologist.

Minutes later an ambulance screamed to an abrupt stop. Astonished that I was alive, the paramedic urged the others to back away as he took charge. The EMT followed close behind spouting instructions into a radio.

"Dispatch; unit 1, our time is 15:58. Call Lifenet. Have them head to the hospital."

Two more ambulances arrived on the scene. The paramedics and EMTs gently rolled me on my back.

At this point, I remember feeling as if I were dreaming. I don't recall the trauma; I simply recognized a flurry of activity and an array of indistinguishable voices. Birds sang, leaves rustled in the breeze, and hard concrete hurt what I thought were sunburned shoulders. Confused, I wondered, *why am I outside?*

"Mrs. Morgan," a man's voice said distinctly, "can you tell me what happened?"

Who is that, and what is he talking about? I thought.

"I...I can't breathe," I said.

The medic noticed a softball-sized hole in front of my left shoulder. It extended deep, through tissue and muscle, exposing blood vessels and bone. He suspected air had seeped into my chest cavity and collapsed my lung. They had to get me to the ambulance immediately.

Doing all they could to keep my arm from falling off as they moved me, the paramedics wrapped a c-collar around my neck and stabilized my body firmly to a backboard. In the ambulance, one of them placed an oxygen mask over my nose and mouth as the other sealed my shoulder the best he could. He inserted a 14 gauge needle between two of my left ribs, and instantly, a puff of air burst from the valve. His hunch was right. I began to breathe easier. Still, time was of the essence. I was going into shock.

"94 to 88, I need a driver over here stat," one of the paramedics blurted into his radio.

At exactly 4:12, Phil watched the ambulance race away with his wife's life in the balance. Suddenly aware of the tension which gripped him, and depleted of the adrenaline that pushed him to ignore it, Phil drew in a deep breath.

"Are you sure you're OK?" an EMT said.

Intense pain in Phil's shoulder consumed him, and everything started to fade. He sat on the concrete barrier and leaned back, starting to faint.

"Whoa!" the EMT said. "Let's get you and your daughters to the hospital."

Phil and the girls arrived at the ER as trauma staff wheeled me in at 4:19. Kayla and Alisha were taken into a closed, soundproof exam room twenty feet from me. Phil occupied an adjacent ER bay to my left, separated only by a curtain. He cringed at each moan and wail of pain.

"Why does it hurt so bad?" I cried.

Unbeknownst to me, my body was covered with intense "road rash." In addition to the huge hole in my shoulder, large hunks of skin and muscle were ripped from the left side of my face and head, exposing my skull. My upper ear was sliced in two. One eye swelled shut, and pieces of my scalp and both eyebrows were gone. Knees, legs, arms...most of the skin that remained was stained black with asphalt.

Doctors and nurses continuously asked me questions to determine the degree of my injuries. When I failed to recollect any details of the crash, they feared the worst – brain injury. Although I seemed coherent and passed all motor, verbal, and eye response tests with a perfect score, amnesia of the accident and a soft swollen spot on the back of my head raised serious concern. Transferring me to a specialized trauma care facility in the city was imminent.

At 4:30 a nurse wheeled me toward the LifeNet helicopter. She paused at Phil's bay. Drawing close to encourage me with a reluctant goodbye, Phil was relieved to see that I recognized him.

"I'll be with you soon," he assured. "Everything's going to be just fine."

Famous last words.

chapter two

Why Would God Let This Happen?

*...you'll never understand the mystery
at work in all that God does.*

ECCLESIASTES 11:5

"Hello?"

Shaken from slumber, Dave Cook swung his feet over the edge of the bed. From his rigid posture and short answers, Allyson could tell this was no annoying sales call.

"I'll be right there," he said, and hung up the phone.

Careful not to disturb the boys napping between them, Allyson propped herself questioningly on one elbow.

"An accident...," Dave said as he hurried from the room. Allyson jumped up and followed him to the front door, hanging on every detail.

"Everyone's alright, but they're air-lifting her to Research."

"Air-lifting who?" Allyson said.

"Pam. Call Alan and tell him to meet me and Phil at the ER."

Dave quickly kissed her and bolted through the door. He jumped into his pickup and sped away, kicking up dust and gravel behind him. Allyson's mind swarmed with questions, but she brushed off the shock and focused on the facts at hand as she dialed the phone. Phil needed help, I needed prayer, and our friends needed to know.

"Hello, Black residence," Brenda answered, drying her hands with a dish towel. Alan didn't even raise an eyebrow from preparing his evening lesson in the next room.

"No..," she said, trailing off into shock.

Alan looked up, and immediately set his notes aside. Seeing the horror on his wife's face, he knew this was more than just church business. Brenda hung up and quickly spilled the news. Alan dropped everything and dashed for his truck. Before the door could slam shut, Brenda reached for the phone again. Her eyes blurred with tears as her trembling fingers dialed the church prayer chain.

"Please, God...please help my friend...," she whispered.

———

"Mrs. Morgan, we are going to fly you to Research Medical Center in Kansas City," a man calmly explained over the whirring thump of the helicopter propeller.

"That sounds like a good idea to me!" I said, still believing this man, this noise, this whole awful thing was just a horrible dream.

———

Meanwhile in Kansas City, Mom and Dad's world shattered. A nurse gave them just enough vague information over the phone to leave them haunted by painful memories. Three years earlier in 1997, Denise – the oldest of my three sisters – died in their home after an exhausting three-year battle with ovarian cancer. In 1998, Denise's only son, Jason, broke his neck while diving into a shallow swimming pool. He survived and narrowly escaped paralysis only for a highway patrolman to show up six months later on Mom and Dad's doorstep, announcing Jason had died in an early morning car accident. Now they feared for their youngest daughter's life as well.

Mom and Dad hurried to the hospital, hoping to meet the

helicopter as it landed. They made it just in time. At 5:22, the Lifenet helicopter nurse rushed my gurney across the helipad. Inside the doors she stopped briefly and gently stroked my face.

"Pam, your parents are here," she said, trying to rouse me from my pain-induced fog.

Mom and Dad couldn't believe what they saw. Mom's comforting face hovered over me. Dad stayed out of sight not wanting me to see the emotion he couldn't hide.

"Hi, Mom," I whispered. "Just pray."

Immediately they rolled me away, and all the fear and horror Mom felt, yet concealed from my eyes, broke loose. She trembled and wept. A nurse gently folded my mother in her arms and guided my distraught parents into a private room.

"I can't believe this is happening again," Mom said.

My sister, Sherry, now the oldest, arrived as trauma team director, Dr. Richard Schnabel, conferred with Mom and Dad.

"I want to see my sister…may I please…now?"

"Certainly," he said, "but only for a few minutes."

Dr. Schnabel led Mom and Sherry to my room. Seeing someone completely unfamiliar lying there, Sherry insisted they must be in the wrong room…until she heard my voice.

"Please pray for me."

Sherry cupped her hand over her mouth, totally unprepared for the mangled mess that was supposed to be her baby sister. Trying to hide her fear, she struggled to compose herself.

"I will," she promised.

Wiping her wet cheeks, Sherry turned to the nurse.

"I want you to see what my sister really looks like," she said, and disappeared.

The nurse handed my wedding ring to my mother. The tear in Mom's heart ripped open a little further as she held it gingerly in her fingers and studied the sparkling marquise-shaped diamond, barely resting in the twisted setting.

In a few minutes Sherry returned, somewhat winded, and handed our current CD, "What Matters Most," to the nurse.

"*This* is my sister."

"Oh, I know her! I've seen them in concert."

Sherry and Mom stayed a few minutes longer while staff prepared to clean my wounds. When everything was ready, they were thoughtfully ushered back to the waiting room. It was hard enough to see a loved one like this without hearing the pain the cleaning process would induce.

As a means of distraction, the nurse strategically chatted with me about my ministry. Still, I cried with each poke as she pried embedded asphalt, rock, and glass from my thigh.

Suddenly, I was quiet. She looked at the clock – 5:58.

"Pam, can you move your toes for me?" she said, noting the change on my chart.

"No..."

Frantic to find the cause, ER staff immediately summoned Dr. Schnabel and scoured through the Bates County transfer records, but everything appeared fine.

"Call neurology! Get Dr. Coufal in here...stat!" Dr. Schnabel commanded.

A machine alarm sounded.

"Her blood pressure is dropping!"

———

Halfway across the country on vacation, my sister, Cynthia, knew something was wrong. She phoned Mom and Dad for the third time from the lobby of her Disneyworld hotel after her husband, Don, insisted she call.

"Why?" she had asked, "We're going home tomorrow. Mom and Dad are picking us up from the airport. We can talk to them then."

"Something just tells me you need to call."

Reluctantly she complied, fully expecting Mom or Dad to answer and tell her everything was just fine. But listening to Dad's voice on the answering machine repeat, "You have reached the Kleeschulte residence...," she had a terrible feeling.

Our accountability group friends felt the same inexplicable urgency at precisely the same time. Jamie and Amy Jones headed into evening worship at six o'clock when an invisible wall seemed to keep them from moving further into the sanctuary. After spending a day in the country, exhaustion could have explained their reluctance, but something told them it was more than that. Jamie and Amy hesitated; both suddenly uncannily aware they weren't supposed to be there. Simultaneously they turned to leave without a word. At home, Allyson's message revealed the secret of their mysterious prompting. Instantly Jamie dropped to his knees and pleaded for my life.

Debbie demanded to see me as she and Rick lugged their three-week-old son's infant carrier into the waiting room in Kansas City.

"No one is allowed at the moment, and when this changes, only *immediate* family," insisted the nurse.

The elder of Denise's two children, my niece, Debbie and I grew close after my sister's death. Her husband and I co-coached her through twenty-two hours of hard labor. And for several days of post-partum at home, I ran errands, did laundry, organized the nursery, and offered advice – tasks my own mother indulged upon me not long ago. Chores of love her mother only dreamed about. Debbie was heartsick over losing her mom and brother in the last three years, and now she grieved the possibility of losing me as well.

Family and friends quickly filled the waiting room to capacity. Among them was our friend and road manager, Barb Underwood.

All sat on the edge of their seats, eager to hear something, yet afraid at the same time. A little after six, Dr. Schnabel pulled the family aside. Obviously in a hurry, his deliberate tone fueled the already mounting anxiety.

"Pam's blood pressure is dropping."

"This can't be happening," Barb said, overhearing. Guilt consumed her. *I should have been there*, she thought. Usually she traveled with us to help set-up, sell CD's, and drive, but today we convinced her to stay home. With our friends there, we had plenty of help and insisted it was the perfect opportunity for Barb to take a well-deserved day off. Now she regretted it. *I could have kept Phil awake*, she thought. *He can't sleep through my incessant chatter!*

Dr. Schnabel offered the services of the hospital Chaplain if our personal minister wasn't available. Gloom descended like a heavy fog. The doctor's unspoken message was heard loud and clear. I might not make it.

Once the doctor left, Sherry's youngest daughter, Dayna, kicked the wall.

"What's wrong with you?" Sherry whispered.

"I can't understand it," Dayna raged. "Why would God let this happen?"

❧ c h a p t e r   t h r e e ❧

Lying in the Dark

*…Let him who walks in the dark,
who has no light, trust in the name of
the LORD and rely on his God.*

ISAIAH 50:10

Many lose themselves in the struggle to understand why bad things happen to loved ones. But Phil's mom seemed to transcend that battle with enormous strength. Madalene walked boldly into Bates County ER. After years of caring for sick and injured family, the surroundings didn't intimidate her in the least.

Like mother, like son. Phil's "Rock of Gibraltar" calm mirrored that of his mom. Phil's collar bone – broken in four places and twisted into a "Z" pattern – shot knives into his shoulder. But in the uncertainty of my condition, he and Madalene were determined to keep the girls confident and secure.

As soon as she turned the corner, Kayla and Alisha ran to Grandma and clung to her. Madalene sighed with relief as the arms of her safe and healthy granddaughters wrapped around her legs. She would have lingered in the moment longer, but time was critical. Phil needed to get moving. He wanted to find the van and trailer before heading to the city.

When the x-rays were reviewed, medications prescribed, and paperwork processed, Madalene gathered the girls and headed home for a long night ahead. She worried about Phil's pain, yet trusted Dave and Alan to take good care of her adult son, and deliver him safely to me, while she comforted her traumatized granddaughters.

Time crawled for my friends and family in Kansas City. At 7:03, Dr. Schnabel returned.

"Pam's blood pressure is stable for the moment," he said, pausing before the bad news, "…but she has lost sensation in her lower extremities. She no longer feels the wounds on her legs, and she can't move her toes. We believe her neck is broken. An MRI will confirm."

As they absorbed the shock of my impending paralysis over the next hour, my blood pressure plummeted again during the MRI. At the neurosurgeon's request, a "swimmer's view" x-ray of my neck from the top down verified Dr. Schnabel's prognosis. My paralysis worsened.

Everyone stared at each other. My condition grew more critical by the hour, and Phil had no idea. Someone needed to call him, but no one wanted to break the bad news. Eyes darted from one to another, and then lowered to the floor. Finally, Barb succumbed.

"I'll call Phil," she said.

As Barb dialed the phone, Phil, Dave and Alan rummaged through the remains of our equipment trailer at Don's APCO in Butler.

The wreckage had been a sobering sight as they pulled into the parking lot. The decrepit van slumped to the left from a missing front wheel. Jagged pieces of glass lined the windshield's perimeter, and the entire driver's side was caved in exposing the hideous scrapes of that treacherous skid across the bridge. A bent accordion shade protruded through the gaping rear side window through which my body flew. Beside the van sat the trailer, its roof propped between. Speakers, mic stands, and plastic bins full of broken CDs and stained-glass crosses were haphazardly stacked on the ground around them. Every piece – a broken fragment of our dream.

Dave and Alan formed an assembly line to arrange everything carefully into the bed of Dave's truck as Phil rummaged through the van.

"Where did I leave my phone?"

A muffled ring reverberated from the console cubby between the front seats. *Of course*, Phil thought, *Pam always puts it in there.* He grabbed the phone and flipped it open.

"Hello?"

"Phil, you've got to get here now!" Barb said.

"Why? Where are you?"

"At Research…"

"What's going on?" he said.

"You've just got to get here…now!"

Barb's unexplained alarm agitated my practical husband. Phil likes to process the facts before deciding how to respond; preferring to act upon his own conclusions instead of someone else's potentially exaggerated, or flawed, perceptions.

"Has Pam died?"

"No…"

Phil sighed with relief.

"Just tell him," he heard Amy whisper in the background.

Barb paused.

"Tell me what?" Phil said.

"They think Pam's neck is broken," she said finally. "Phil…she might not make it."

Dave and Alan overheard Barb on the other end of the phone. Immediately they stopped what they were doing, their faces turning pale as they nervously awaited Phil's instruction. Transferring equipment no longer seemed important, at least not now. Phil flipped the phone shut.

"My wife may have a broken neck. She may not make it through the night. I kinda want to get there," he said.

"We're going *now*!" Alan blurted.

"Go on," Dave said, "I'll load all this into my garage and wait by the phone."

And they were off. Phil jumped into Alan's truck as he peeled out of the station lot. *If a police officer stops me for speeding*, Alan thought, *I'll get an escort.*

Phil stared pensively through the passenger window. Suddenly, Alan broke out in prayer. He begged for safety and swiftness in travel. He urged for Phil's strength of heart. He pleaded for my life and healing. He implored for the doctors to be skilled, compassionate, gentle, and thorough.

Shaving a typical hour's drive to a record 25 minutes, Alan and Phil walked into Research Medical Center's ER waiting room at 9:00 p.m.

My family congregated at one end of the room, and our friends at the other. Each face turned expectantly to my husband. Small pockets of people exchanged worried, hushed words, while anxiety and grief stifled most of my family. They didn't know how much he knew, and feared saying the wrong thing.

Phil interpreted their silence to mean blame and migrated toward the comforting hugs and safety of his friends. But with each passing moment the awkwardness grew, until Phil finally confronted the situation.

"I fell asleep," he calmly announced. "Please, let's not blame anyone, let's just pray."

To my husband's relief, everyone formed a circle and clasped hands, agreeing that bitterness, resentment, and blame had no place. All uncertainty and potential animosity toward Phil dissolved as his honest and bold prayer of faith united each heart. A chorus of tearful amen's resounded.

In the silence that followed, the ticking wall clock read 10:30. Phil encouraged everyone to go home. I had been moved to ICU in critical yet stable condition, and he promised to call if anything changed. Reluctantly the crowd dwindled until only immediate family and Alan remained. Lingering with his friend a few minutes longer, Phil let out a long sigh as the weight of his world bore down.

"On top of everything else, I think I'm out of a job," he said.

Alan let out a slight empathetic chuckle, identifying well with Phil's burden. "God will provide, my friend. God will provide."

Appreciating the gentle reminder, Phil hugged Alan as he turned to leave. Then he sank back into a chair beside Mom, Dad and Sherry to await the MRI results.

Finally at midnight, neurosurgeon Dr. Frank Coufal introduced himself and led them into the MRI suite. A shocking image of my neck revealed a complete dislocation between the sixth and seventh cervical vertebrae which pulled and pinched my spinal cord into a detrimental "S" shape. Mom and Sherry gasped. Dr. Coufal explained that I was in traction. Screws in my temples fastened to a metal frame encircling my head which attached at the top to a thick metal cable holding ten pounds of weight. The intention was, in essence, to stretch, straighten, and realign the vertebrae to their proper position.

As tenderly as possible, Dr. Coufal interpreted my condition into words my grieved family could understand. First, the good news: no brain injury. The soft spot of original concern was merely a concussion that would pass – a true blessing in light of what happened. But he hated to break the bad news. Paralysis that began in my feet and legs ascended to my shoulders. Traction successfully restored the use of my arms, and he administered medication to reduce the swelling of the cord, but the damage was already done. The location and severity of the injury permanently and irrevocably traumatized the spinal cord rendering me quadriplegic. Never again would I feel or move anything from the chest down, including my fingers. In a bed or wheelchair the rest of my days, life as we knew it forever changed.

Weary and in pain, Phil found the details hard to process at this late hour. But he chose to zone in on the good news – no brain injury.

"There have been blessings all the way through this," he said.

"Well, I sure want to know what the blessings are in *this*!" Mom said.

"Mom!" Sherry chastised, embarrassed by the unexpected retort from her typically gentle and meek mother. "The *blessing* is that she is still *alive!*"

Hours of worry, fear, anger, and uncertainty were simply too much for my mama to handle, especially considering her previous three years. While Phil held on to any minuscule measure of good news, Mom heard only the pain.

Sherry and Dad decided to go home. Determined to stay, Mom and Phil were directed to accommodations in a nearby nurse's dorm. Wandering down the lonely hall, Mom's familiar tenderness returned as Phil's medication wore off and pain quickly overwhelmed him. She snagged a stray wheelchair lingering in the corridor and urged him to sit. As she pushed, Phil seized the opportunity to explain and hopefully return the comfort.

"Judy, God has been with us all the way through this," Phil said.

Mom sighed as if surrendering. "I know, you've said as much, but please…tell me what you mean."

He unraveled the amazing details of what took place, the cars that stopped, and the lives that were spared, including mine. Mom couldn't deny God's hand. Still, she struggled with her inability to protect me from the agony and difficulty ahead.

Finding a room and stretching out on the mattress, Phil decided to keep his uneasiness about this new twist in his life to himself. He replayed the day from beginning to end, and twenty-four hours seemed like a lifetime. The day began weary, yet promising, as the sun ascended over the horizon. Now lying in the dark, it ended way beyond weary, with today's promise fading into tomorrow's unknown.

Broken and Ruined

*A bruised reed he will not break, and a
smoldering wick he will not snuff out.*

ISAIAH 42:3

"What happened?" I asked, noticing the sling around Phil's shoulder.

I thought I roused from a long nap and expected to hear the familiar hum of tires on the highway and see the plush mauve interior of our cozy conversion van. Instead, sterile hospital chrome and drab green walls stared back at me. I didn't remember anything after falling asleep next to Kayla. Momentary flashes in the helicopter and ER all seemed like a bad dream. Finally, I understood. This was no dream.

"We've been in an accident," Phil said, rather mechanically. "I fell asleep, and we hit a guardrail. The van flipped over, and you were thrown out. I broke my collar-bone from the seat belt."

Phil patiently answered the question again, as he had all morning. My brain had refused to register his words, until now.

"It's not your fault," I said, my heart breaking, "it could easily have been me behind that wheel…"

"I know," he said and smiled, realizing by the change in conversation my mental condition had improved. "Don't worry about me."

Phil had already won the battle with blame and guilt, and I was thankful. They had no place between us. I didn't care what happened or why; I only cared that he stood safely beside me.

Suddenly, my pulse raced as I scanned the room. "Where are the girls?"

"They are fine and at home with my mom," Phil soothed.

A tidal wave of relief swept over me. "Oh, thank God!"

"Just rest," he said. "Don't worry; I'm here."

Gladly taking his advice, I drifted back into dreamland; certain that we would be home together soon. In reality, my body resembled something out of a horror movie. And as I slept, orthopedic surgeon, Dr. Jeffrey Weaver, and plastic surgeon, Dr. Joseph Cannova, Jr., prepped for the first of many surgeries on my long road to recovery. I wouldn't see home again for a long time.

The wheels of my gurney rolled into the OR as the wheels of my sister's plane touched down on the other side of town.

Completely clueless to the past day's events, Cynthia emerged from the jet-way expecting to see Mom, but instead spotted Sherry, waiting with Dad outside the gate.

Mom didn't want to leave me, so Sherry decided to accompany Dad to the airport, deciding it best if she broke the news. Dad's tenderness often overpowers his "got-it-together" exterior. Sherry wanted to save Daddy from the pain of re-living this nightmare once again, as well as the embarrassment of breaking down in public.

Cynthia flung her arms around Sherry, pleasantly surprised to see her sister. But her cheerful expression quickly changed to suspicion.

"Why aren't you at work? And by the way, where's Mom?"

Just then, Cynthia recognized Sherry's strained smile. Sherry always had a hard time keeping secrets, and from the look on her face now, she hadn't changed. Cynthia was certain that she and

Don's uneasiness in Florida had been a premonition.

"What's going on?" she said, anxiety sweeping over her again. "Where's Mom?"

"Everything is fine," Sherry said, managing to place a smile in her voice. "Mom is watching the girls for Phil and Pam, and I didn't want Dad to drive alone."

The sick feeling inside Cynthia wouldn't budge. Sherry's story didn't quite match her nonverbal message that something was wrong...really wrong. Why wouldn't her sister confess? Dad was quiet, but that wasn't unusual. Cynthia pressed again as they walked toward the car, and Sherry insisted more adamantly that everything was "just fine." So Cynthia gave up, convinced that she misinterpreted what was going on.

As Dad pulled away from the parking lot, Cynthia started to chat about the weather in Florida and how crowded Disney World was and...

"Dad and I have something we need to tell you," Sherry interrupted. Dad began to cry silently. "Pam has been in an accident."

"What?" Cynthia whispered, trembling.

"Everything is going to be fine. They say she's going to make it."

Sherry sounded as though she wanted to convince herself as well as her sister. Tearfully she unveiled the uncertain details of my injuries and paralysis. Cynthia fell apart. All the apprehension brewing in her heart over the last twenty-four hours finally released.

———~ᔕᔕᔕ~———

Back at the hospital, Dr. Weaver and Dr. Cannova surgically debrided and completely assessed my bones and joints. When they finally emerged to debrief my family, Dr. Weaver spoke first.

Going into surgery his concerns were twofold: first, he worried that I could lose all shoulder and knee function if the joints were compromised. Yet, the risk of "contamination" disturbed him even more. Ideally, cleaning and closing the wounds is done right away, but because of the instability of my neck injury, surgical debridement had to wait. The delay most likely caused infection to settle into my joints and deep tissue, especially considering bits and pieces of bacteria-ridden roadside were embedded into my flesh. Such serious contamination often required amputation, or in the worst of cases, proved fatal.

Both doctors appeared amazed. In spite of the deep surface mutilation, no other bones besides my neck were broken. My shoulder and knee joints remained intact *and* – to top it all off – no sign of infection could be found! Extensive ligament and tendon damage surrounded my right knee, but in light of my paralysis, it wasn't worth further trauma to fix.

Everyone breathed a sigh of relief.

Dr. Cannova seemed pleased as well. The deltoid muscle of my left shoulder was destroyed, but the doctor saw hope for the softball-sized crater that remained in its absence. With additional surgery, the plastic surgeon could split the pectoral muscle in my chest and rotate it around to cover the vacant space.

"Pam's shoulder has complex lacerations, and I will need to perform extensive tissue transfer," he said, "but with skin grafts and muscle re-arrangement, she should regain most, if not all, of the motion in her left arm."

That was the good news. The doctor's tune changed as he described how difficult it was to find enough healthy skin to graft. He discovered a patch on my upper left thigh protected by my shorts that would cover my forearm and shoulder, but it wouldn't work on my face.

"Only facial skin can replace facial skin effectively," Dr. Cannova said, "even skin on the neck is too ruddy for the face."

Dr. Cannova zeroed in on the massive mutilation to my face alone. A silver dollar-sized hole lay in the middle of my forehead and a much larger one – four to five times its size – on the left side of my face. He stretched my cheek as much as he could, but it wouldn't go very far. I was too young and thin to have enough extra skin for such a large area. It would require a series of surgeries, and even then, he feared drastic disfigurement.

"My only choice is to use skin from her scalp," he said.

"Will hair grow on her face?" Phil said.

"No, only the top layers are used. They don't contain hair follicles. As soon as I receive clearance from neurology, I'll schedule the procedure."

Phil took the news calmly – a little too calmly for the doctor's comfort. Dr. Cannova didn't seem to understand or appreciate my husband's composure under such dire circumstances. He eased in for a private word, looking Phil directly in the eyes.

"Pam is going to look bad for a long time," he said bluntly, his words chastising. "She is going to need your support. I'll do as much as I can, but the intensity of her wounds will forever change her appearance. Are you okay with this?"

Phil didn't hesitate, "Yes, I'm fine."

Tuesday I met Dr. Patel, a kind man of Indian descent, who was in charge of my rehabilitation. He spoke with a slight accent.

"Pam, I'm going to test your sensation by lightly poking you with this pin," he said. "I want you to tell me when you feel it."

Starting at my feet, Dr. Patel slid his arm under the sheet, careful not to let me see where he poked. Occasionally I felt slight pressure against my skin as he ascended to my arms and torso. When he reached my upper chest, I felt a sharp *Prick!*

"Ouch!"

"Sorry!" Dr. Patel said, and turned to his young intern, "She has a C4 bib."

The pretty brunette wrote it down.

"What does that mean?" I asked.

I'm not particularly oriented to science, and the fuzzy effects of morphine didn't help, so I'm still not exactly sure what it meant. All I know is that it meant I had normal sensation inside the area a bib would cover around my neck.

Dr. Patel explained we have two sets of nerves that run parallel to each other – motor nerves and sensory nerves. Motor nerves control the body's movement. I could bend my right arm which indicated normal bicep function, but I had weak triceps, completely limp fingers, and I couldn't move anything from my chest down.

"Your motor damage is at the C6 level," Dr. Patel said. "and the pin test tells me your sensory damage is at the C7 level."

Normal sensation in my upper chest decreased significantly as he moved the pin to the side and down my arm. At my fingers, I felt the sharp needle prick my thumb, but it became blunter with each finger until the sensation disappeared completely at my pinky. Dr. Patel scribbled his report in my records.

"Complete SCI - ASIA A" – a diagnosis carrying a life-changing sentence none of us could yet comprehend.

Spinal cord injuries are defined as either complete or incomplete. According to research, complete injuries produce total loss of all motor and sensory function below the level of injury. Neither a complete nor incomplete injury guarantees any functional return of strength or sensation, but an incomplete injury carries a measure of hope. A complete does not. Usually complete injuries carry a life sentence of permanent, irreparable paralysis. Less than 5% recover, and if the classification is maintained 72 hours after the initial injury, recovery is essentially zero.[1]

The American Spinal Injury Association (ASIA) further classifies spinal cord injuries into five categories, A-E. "A" is the most severe and is determined by absence of sensory and motor function in the lowest sacral areas.[2] That was me.

I didn't know the severity of my spinal cord injury at the time, and my family intended to keep it that way, at least for the time being. I needed to rest. What I didn't know wouldn't hurt me, as the old saying goes, so they were my shield, protecting me from fear as long as they could.

Wednesday night I opened my eyes from morphine's trance to find Mom and Sherry standing beside me on opposite sides of my bed. Still under the assumption my condition wasn't that serious, I was pleasantly surprised to see Sherry. My petite blonde sister's compassion was comforting.

"What are you doing here?"

"I just wanted to see you," she said.

"Oh, hey, your birthday is next week. Let's do lunch, OK?"

Sherry's deep blue eyes clouded with concern. "O…kay…," she said slowly. "How are you feeling?"

"Okay," I said. "The sunburn I got yesterday really hurts."

Sherry's eyes met Mom's with a glance that said, "She doesn't have any idea what's going on, does she?"

"That's not a sunburn…" Sherry began.

Although we talked for quite a while about my "road rash" and debridement, I don't remember the discussion at all. Sherry says I insisted to see the damage for myself, and although she hesitated, the nurse encouraged her to hold a mirror so that I could see my reflection. Reluctantly, Sherry obliged and watched me carefully survey each gory detail with a detached, analytical eye, as if examining a science project. I don't remember any of it.

All I recall was the rotating bed. Still in traction, my body and head were restrained, secured by large foam wedges in a monstrous green rotating bed which rolled from side to side like a huge teeter-totter. It was supposed to help my circulation, but it didn't do much for conversation. As we talked, Sherry suddenly disappeared.

"Where did you go?"

"I'm still here," she said. "Your bed rotates."

Confused, I grew frustrated.

"You're going to have surgery tomorrow morning," Mom said, and calmly explained the upcoming procedure to fuse my neck, soothing my alarm.

The safety I always felt in her presence as a child returned and instilled confidence that everything would be okay. Mom simply wouldn't have it any other way.

"Will you wake me before I go, so I can see you first?"

Mom smiled and nodded as I drifted off once more.

The next morning Dr. Coufal described the fragile task that lay before him.

Although the traction re-aligned my spine successfully, he wasn't sure how severely my spinal cord had been damaged. Additional testing was too perilous. Because of this, he couldn't determine his exact course of action, or how long it would take, but he did emphasize the chance of further injury. Working closely to the spinal cord always presented the risk. Up to this point, I reported consistent tingling in my toes when touched, but he couldn't say if this would continue. Still, Dr. Coufal tried to sound hopeful.

As Phil waited for me to be taken down to the OR, the surgical nurse introduced herself.

"You probably don't remember me, but I saw you sing recently," she said with a sympathetic smile. "The operating room is full of praying Christians, and I brought the CD I bought at your concert to play during surgery."

Phil was amazed. What were the odds of this particular nurse seeing us in concert a few weeks before? It was just the encouragement Phil needed to remember God was in control during the next eight hours of uncertainty.

Delicate surgery revealed four broken cervical vertebrae instead of the expected two. Dr. Coufal removed six centimeters of hip bone to reconstruct and secure my neck and to fuse C4-C7 together with four screws and a titanium plate. The surgery left a large zipper-like scar down the back of my lower neck, extending between my shoulder blades.

After surgery I vaguely recall waking in recovery to the sound of two unfamiliar young men discussing some KU sport at the foot of my bed. One of them was a nurse's aid; the other – my night-shift nurse, Paul, whose attentive care quickly made him one of my favorites.

I heard a whooshing rhythmic sound, and felt pressure in my throat and heaviness in my chest. I couldn't inhale at will, and I couldn't speak. Out of the corner of my eye, I saw the source of the puzzling sound – a ventilator. A strange-looking cylinder with an accordion-like apparatus inside expanded and collapsed at regular, slow intervals. A sudden rush of adrenaline compelled me to gasp as I realized this thing was breathing for me.

I'm not sure if an alarm sounded, or if Paul's uncanny, built-in radar simply tuned in to the fear in my eyes. His friendly face immediately appeared over mine.

"Would you like something to help you sleep, Mrs. Morgan?" he asked, already administering a sedative.

I remained "vented" and sedated for four days until the bulk of my surgeries were complete. This was a slight alteration to protocol, but inserting and removing the breathing tube numerous times during a short period of time could damage my vocal cords, so they thought it best. Thankfully, constant sedation eliminated additional panic attacks.

Fusing my neck fared much better than Dr. Coufal anticipated. On the MRI, my spinal cord was twisted, pulled, stretched out of shape, and appeared to be pinched off in two places. He never saw anyone live with an injury so severe. Yet, in surgery he found the spinal cord and surrounding layer of protective fluid still intact.

Phil's eyes lit up when he heard the doctor's report. He praised God, convinced I would recover and walk again.

Dr. Coufal didn't count on it, and his colleagues agreed. He warned Phil not to get his hopes up. Severe stretching and bruising caused irreparable damage. It was the worst dislocation of the neck he had ever seen.

Nevertheless, Dr. Coufal said the final say was yet to come. I was currently in spinal shock, a result of spinal cord swelling after an injury. This condition usually faded in three days after which feeling and movement would slowly return if I were to recover. The doctor made no promises. Phil needed to face reality, he said.

"Your wife is destined to be a quadriplegic."

---

1 www.emedicine.com/EMERG/topic553.htm - pg. 12 of 15.
2 www.emedicine.com/pmr/topic182.htm - pg. 2 of 9, and www.sci-info-pages.com/levels.html

chapter five

What Would I Do Without You?

...come quickly to me, O God.
You are my help and my deliverer...

PSALMS 70:5

Quadriplegic...face reality...the final say. Phil understood the doctor's words. Yet another post-surgical report defied medical reason. How was it possible after what they saw on the MRI that my spinal cord wasn't severed or even punctured?

A comforting song by The Isaacs Family suddenly played in Phil's head. He'd heard it several times on the radio that week since the accident.

They don't know the God I serve
already knows the answers,
They don't know He still works miracles
and holds us in His hands.
Man may give his best opinion
on what the future holds,
But I look up for my solution,
for they don't know what God knows.

- WRITTEN BY SONYA ISAACS[1]

Phil understood the doctors wanted him to face the reality of their experience. After all, they see these things all the time. But God's miracles were also reality; the Bible is full of them, and he had personally seen amazing evidence. Dr. Coufal was right about one thing. The final say *was* yet to come, and God would have it. That, Phil believed.

My husband determined I would believe it, too. When I first realized I couldn't feel or move I was horrified. Yet, Phil's faith and confidence calmed me.

"You can't feel or move anything right now," he said, "but don't worry, you will."

Phil's unrelenting conviction that I would walk again kept me going, and kept our friends and family from falling apart. He absolutely refused to lose hope. After each surgery or new examination report, Phil looked for the positive. He separated actualities from potentialities and emphasized the futility of stressing over the latter, always praying and thanking God for His blessings.

Prayer was paramount. Phil sent e-mails almost daily to over 500 ministry followers with a request for mass petition to God's throne. Thanks to modern technology, the news spread like wildfire. Over the next several weeks, we received thousands of e-mails and cards with sincere, heartfelt prayers for complete healing from coast to coast and all over the world...Guam, Poland, Canada...

On Monday, June 12, just eight days into this nightmare, Phil wrote, "Keep praying!!! God is working and He's not finished yet. I'm excited to see the good God is going to bring out of this difficult time. I'm convinced He's going to use us in a bigger way than we ever dreamed..."

Phil believed; he just wished God would hurry up and get on with it. More than three days since my neurosurgery, I was off the ventilator, and Dr. Coufal confirmed his prognosis of my complete and permanent paralysis. My "window of hope" waned without a flicker of sensation or movement. Each doctor recorded the same result in my chart, "No response."

Wednesday dawned with a glimmer of hope. I awoke to

a familiar sound...the steady drone of a hair dryer. Part of the regimen in caring for my skin grafts called for applying heat to the gauze-covered donor sites on my thigh. This morning, my nurse solicited Phil's help with her routine. He set the dryer on high and held it in one spot over my leg while watching the Today show on the television hanging from the ceiling in the corner.

"What are you doing?" I said.

"I'm not sure," Phil said, not taking his eyes from the screen, "the nurse told me to do this."

"Well, move it around, it's hot!"

"Really?" Phil suddenly forgot the TV and snapped the hairdryer away from my leg, beaming with surprise and promise.

His hopes soared, but soon disintegrated when later that day I made a disturbing change. I slept more than usual, and seemed detached and disoriented when awake. Nothing I said made sense.

Phil and Mom quietly discussed my mental stability with a nurse across the room. Usually the sound of family in the room comforted me as I rested, but not today. Their chatter annoyed me. Gradually their volume increased as they approached my bedside.

"Do you know where you are?" my nurse asked.

"Yes. In the hospital." My answer was slow and unsure.

"Do you know which one?"

"Yes...," I said. "I...had my babies here."

"That's right," she said, and pointed at Phil. "Do you know who this is?"

"Well, of course!" I said, and then paused to think. *How ridiculous*, I thought in a cloudy haze, *I wish they would let me sleep.*

I drifted off, and Phil waited several long, agonizing seconds before I opened my eyes again.

"He's...my... husband."

"Can you tell me his name?"

Phil smiled lovingly, and I knew that I couldn't love anyone on earth as much, but...what was his name? Several more silent seconds passed, and my drooping eyelids closed in deep sleep.

Phil immediately felt sick to his stomach. Dr. Coufal initially reported no brain injury, but maybe his diagnosis was premature. *She couldn't say my name,* he thought. Paralysis and disfigurement wouldn't be easy, but not having the woman he fell in love with...the woman who listened to him, understood him, laughed at his jokes, and shared his hopes and dreams... Phil pondered the possibilities, and he began to hurt.

The next several hours limped by as he waited for the doctor's assessment. Seeking a word of encouragement, Phil discovered an e-mail message from George Moore, the associate pastor of our church.

> *A few hours ago I was at the bedside of an amazing young woman who has been seriously injured and for whom the prognosis is still uncertain. But even as I stood there, I felt the warmth of Pam's faith and personality blessing me, and the others about her bedside. We even chuckled together about her itching nose. With a host of injuries, the most frustrating thing at the moment was an itch that Pam could not deal with and others could not seem to find.*
>
> *Only God knows how many lives your ministry has touched, and now how many people are lifting you in prayer to the Great Physician.*
>
> *A long time ago I read a line attributed to another Methodist preacher, Ralph Soxman. He said: 'An accident is something that persons cannot foresee, and that God did not intend.' I have found that personally helpful in coming to grips with calamities such as yours. But the wonderful sequel to that is found in the words of Paul: 'God is at work for good in all things for those who love the Lord.'*
>
> *You both have shown amazing strength in this ordeal, but accept that you don't always have to be strong, because God always will be!*

Phil read Pastor George's message again, closed his eyes, and allowed the encouragement to sink in. He was lost in thought when Dr. Schnabel walked through the door.

The trauma doctor believed my disorientation to merely be the result of changing pain medications. I received powerful doses of two different pain meds rather close together. Still, only time would tell. When the drugs wore off and I awoke, they would know for sure.

Phil sat in a corner chair and glanced at his watch. "God, please, let the doctor be right," he prayed.

Hearing a stir in the room, I opened my eyes, "Phil?"

He bolted from the chair to my side.

"Hey, there you are," I said. "I love you."

Relief and gratitude welled up in Phil's eyes. He covered my hand with his.

"I've been thinking," he said. "All that matters is that we're still together. This isn't your injury, it's our injury, and we're gonna make it through this with God's help."

"I'm so blessed to have you," I whispered. Tears spilled from my eyes, their warmth streaming down my cold cheeks. Phil brushed their trail aside with his finger.

"What would I do without you?" I said.

1 "They Don't Know What God Knows" written by Sonya Isaacs. ©1998 Isaacs Family Publishing, Pisgah Ridge Music, BMI. Used by permission. From the Horizon Records CD "The Isaacs - Increase My Faith"

Waking Up to Reality

O LORD, hear my prayer, listen to
my cry for mercy; in your faithfulness and
righteousness come to my relief.

PSALM 143:1

Pneumonia is the single leading cause of death in spinal cord injury victims. Doctors did everything they could to keep me from compounding the statistic. Yet when my temperature spiked and the doctor ordered a chest x-ray, my family received the troublesome news: Mucus completely plugged my left lung.

Immediately the doctor placed me on intense antibiotics, breathing treatments every four hours, and inhalation exercises every hour. But coughing was the key to kicking this thing. Unfortunately, what sounded easy enough was horribly frightening.

My chest felt bound as if squeezed by a tight band. With a paralyzed diaphragm, my breathing was shallow, sneezes virtually inaudible, and speaking reduced mostly to a whisper. Coughing came close to impossible.

Nurses instructed Phil and Mom to push my stomach each time I tried to cough, but phlegm often collected in my throat and blocked my airway causing me to choke and panic. I hated it. I did everything I could to keep from coughing. Big mistake.

Pulmonary stepped in to perform a bronchoscopy. What a

nightmare! Simply put, they wanted to vacuum my lungs. A sweet lady technician inched a tube up my nose and down my throat, watching the probe's path on a television monitor. The ventilator was merely a foreshadow of the suffocating terror I experienced as that skinny little hose penetrated my lungs and sucked up everything in it's path. No sedation was offered to deliver me from the anxiety. On the contrary, I remained wide awake.

"Hang in there," she coached as I gagged, "this won't take long."

That, I thought, was her opinion. It seemed like an eternity to me. From then on, I vowed to do whatever it took to keep that thing away from me. I just didn't realize that it entailed the ruthless, depriving misery of extreme thirst.

A swallowing test determined I wasn't swallowing properly – probably the reason I got pneumonia in the first place. A glorious sip of grape juice most likely drained straight into my lungs.

That settled it. Thin liquids, even ice chips, were out of the question. My only option was to thicken water or juice with a powdered gelatin-like substance. Disgusting doesn't come close to describing that stuff. It was absolutely awful, and made me thirstier than ever.

I couldn't stand it. How bad could ice chips be? They melted slowly. Surely I could manage swallowing a little bit of water at a time. Growing desperate, I played dumb during shift changes and politely requested ice, hoping the new nurse had yet to review my chart. I prayed for repeat nurses to forget, and if they didn't, I blamed my lapse in memory on the morphine.

One time I succeeded, but only momentarily. A sweet ICU nurse brought the cold squares of crystal heaven to my room and fed me a chip or two before leaving to be debriefed by the previous nurse. I relished their moist refreshment until she returned mere minutes later to whisk them away. So much for that.

This seems funny to me now, and at the time gave my friends and family something to smile about during a dangerously precarious situation, but I didn't feel like smiling then. My helpless captivity drove me crazy. When I was awake, I couldn't escape. I couldn't avoid the fear that sponge baths, linen changes, or 6 a.m. chest x-rays invoked. Unable to help or support myself in any way, every move brought excruciating pain and frightening instability. I couldn't rid myself of the annoying feeding tube that rubbed my nose raw. I couldn't reposition my pillows. I couldn't adjust the rigid, uncomfortable neck brace. I couldn't ...I couldn't....I couldn't.

Phil and Mom alternated days with me in the ICU, but weren't allowed to stay the night. I dreaded to see them leave. I wanted someone with me constantly. What if an eyelash fell into my eye, if I got an itch, if I needed to cough...?

Anxiety settled in my stomach – the sickening, heavy sense of an ever-present cloud of fearful dread and worry. I never felt so alone. *No one could possibly understand how I feel,* I thought. I had to depend on someone else for *everything.*

For the first time in my life, I wanted to die. Crushing grief saturated my soul. I wished God had just taken me home with Him, instead of leaving me here like this.

Phil did everything he could think of to help me feel better. To me, he was a saint. Knowing how I missed the girls, he snuck Kayla into the ICU. He knew I needed to see her sweet face as much as she needed to see that I was still alive.

Kayla remembered the bridge at the accident scene and was certain I had fallen into the water. Everyone insisted I was okay, but she needed to see for herself.

Kayla hesitantly walked in with her round eyes fixed on me. Daddy rested his soothing hand on her shoulder and encouraged her with each step. As she approached my bedside, my heart ached. My brave little girl faced the frightening sight of her mommy terribly battered. Her eyes were the only mirror that told me how bad it must appear. I wanted her to crawl in next to me. I wanted to stroke her hair, feel the silkiness of her skin against my cheek, and hold her tight, but I couldn't. My wounded arm lay limp at my side.

Seeing her motivated me to put aside my self-pity, at least for the moment. With all the faith I could muster, I resolved to alleviate my precious baby's fears and convince her of my recovery.

"Mommy needs some extra special care for awhile," I said, "but before long, we will all be together as a family again."

Her eyes scanned my body, taking in the bandages, tubes, and exposed wounds.

"I know I look a little scary right now, and when I get home, things may be different for a while. But what really matters is that we still have each other. I love you, Sweetheart!"

"I love you, too, Mommy!" she said quietly.

The next morning I emerged from morphine's oblivion with Kayla and Alisha on my mind. Who knew when I could see my babies again? And when I did.....then what?

All the things I used to do in their lives played through my head: kneeling beside the tub, crawling and rolling around on the floor, changing diapers, washing clothes, scratching backs, flying kites, pushing their swings, rocking them to sleep, fixing macaroni and cheese, shopping for groceries, doctoring boo-boos, hugging them close to my chest...the busy duties and joys of being a Mommy.

I envisioned hair-tousled Alisha running to me with raised arms begging, "Hold me, Mommy!" I pictured Kayla, wrapped in her hooded white bath towel, waiting for me to pick her up and cradle her in my arms singing, "Rock-a-bye Baby," as we always did after bath-time.

The long-term impact of my paralysis began to sink in and created an aching pit of emptiness inside me. By the time Phil arrived, I was a mess. He tried lifting my spirits with his witty sense of humor, but to no avail.

Stopping by for a quick visit before work, Barb found Phil wiping tears from my eyes.

"I can't be a mommy like this," I said.

Barb set her purse down and approached my bed with firm determination in her voice.

"You, my dear, are the only mother these girls have, and the only one they need, paralyzed or not," she insisted. "Being a mother is not about what you can do for them, but in what you teach them and how much you love them. You are doing that right here, right now."

Barb's emphatic, wise counsel soothed my misgivings down for the time being. But my heart still ached.

———— ✧ ————

After nearly two weeks, I moved out of ICU into Acute Care on the fourth floor. In my new environment, Phil and Mom were allowed to stay in my room overnight. Phil split his time between me and the girls. One day and night husband, the next, daddy.

I felt so much better to finally have someone with me around the clock. I felt safe. And it helped pass the time. More and more, I roused back to a consistent awareness of life in the real world – a different world where uncertainty, discomfort, and struggle dominated.

Phil and I looked forward to spending our first night together in the same room, but I couldn't sleep. My head itched terribly. Daily sponge baths didn't include washing my hair, and after two weeks, I'd had enough. Built up oil and wound creams greased my scalp, and even though Barb had spent hours trying to pick them out, clumps of dried blood, asphalt, and glass still clung like glue. Phil called the nurse.

"Would you like me to wash your hair?" a young, pleasant nurse asked. This wasn't her normal floor assignment, but she was eager to help.

"Can you do that? I mean, with my neck and everything?"

"Sure we can."

Calling two other nurses to assist, they supported my neck and maneuvered my head over a portable sink. I purred like a kitten as they shampooed my hair and loosened the knotted mess. What a relief!

The following morning was Sunday, and I felt like rejoicing. I had so many reasons to be thankful. Out of ICU with clean hair, I ate a few bites of applesauce for breakfast. My pneumonia was improving and my wounds were healing nicely according to Dr. Cannova. In fact, the following day he planned to graft skin from the top of my head to the side of my face – if everything went well, my final hurdle before moving to rehab. But the best news by far was the promise of sitting in a wheelchair by Wednesday or Thursday.

Obviously I couldn't go to church, so Barb and Phil brought church to me. They read scripture and prayed with me. I felt refreshed and uplifted as we concluded our worship with a few lines from one of Phil's songs. It was always one of my favorites, especially now...

> *...when troubles come and knock me to my knees,*
> *the only hope I have is the only hope I need.*[1]

I headed into the arctic atmosphere of the operating room early Monday relying on that hope. I wasn't sure if I trembled because of the cold air or because of my nerves. I hadn't been this lucid before any of my previous surgeries. On one hand, I was eager for Dr. Cannova to fix my face, yet I was scared to death at the same time. A nurse tucked a heated blanket around me to warm my shivering body. As she rolled me into the OR, a song from our CD, "God Chooses Who He Uses" permeated the air.

I couldn't believe it. *How cool is this?* I thought.

Dr. Cannova, scrubbed and gloved, peered over his mask with smiling eyes.

"Is that you?" he said, nodding in the direction of the music.

"That's me!"

> *God chooses who He uses to do mighty deeds.*
> *The broken and ruined are all that He needs.*
> *It's not by your merit what you do or say.*
> *God chooses who He uses to do His will His way.*[2]

Numerous nurses, technicians, and doctors were clearly moved by the irony. I recognized it in their smiles and in their eyes. My voice was singing, but God was the one speaking to *everyone* in the room, including me. As the anesthetic took effect, I felt completely at peace.

Little did I know that twenty-four hours later this peace would again fade into fear.

First thing Tuesday a coughing fit seized me after my 6:00 a.m. chest x-ray. It wasn't unusual, and typically relaxed within a few minutes. This time, however, it didn't. Before long, I grew short of breath.

Phil rested on his roll-away cot by the window.

"Phil! Call the nurse!" I urged between coughs.

He roused and pressed the button, but the nurse didn't come.

"You'll be OK, just cough that junk up and get it out of there!" he said, and rolled over, wanting to go back to sleep.

"I...(cough)...can't breathe!"

"You're scheduled for a breathing treatment in twenty minutes," Phil soothed.

"I need someone NOW!"

Phil finally realized the urgency. He jumped up and ran out of the room, quickly returning with a nurse. My temperature had risen and my blood oxygen level dropped to 83%. Immediately the nurse placed an urgent page to Dr. Schnabel and within minutes, I was headed back to ICU.

The ICU nurse opened the oxygen tank to full capacity, and placed a mask over my nose and mouth. The blast of cold, damp air against my face made me shiver, but I didn't care.

"Breathe deep, Pam," she said.

I drank it in.

Over the next several hours my anxiety slowly subsided as my oxygen level crept back to normal levels. Finally, I could breathe.

Dr. Schnabel feared he would find a pulmonary embolism, but he didn't see any clots on my morning chest x-ray. To confirm, he ordered an MRI.

The same radiologist was on duty who administered my first MRI that horrible night in the ER.

"You look much better than the last time I saw you," she said.

I apologized for not remembering her. I didn't remember anything from that night.

"Good thing," the radiologist said. "Your neck brace pushes on your ears and since we couldn't remove it, we couldn't get the earplugs in. Now, keep your head very still."

Carefully she removed my neck brace (which terrified me) and poked an ear plug into each ear. As the testing began, I soon understood what she meant. In spite of the earplugs, a horrific clatter of knocking and buzzing filled the small tubular cavern my body occupied. I couldn't believe I didn't remember this.

Dr. Schnabel said the initial readings appeared normal, but a specialist's second opinion discovered small, peripheral clots in my lungs, virtually undetectable to the untrained eye. These sly curdles of blood held deadly potential. Knocking them loose could allow them to make a fatal trip to my heart.

Administering blood thinner early on usually keeps paralyzed victims' blood from forming clots that can travel to the lungs and heart, but the intensity of my wounds and impending surgeries made thinning my blood too dangerous. I could have bled to death. Now it was the only option. For seven days I had to lie flat until the clots safely dissolved.

Two long and lonely nights in the ICU followed. It was hard to keep worry outside the door. I longed to sleep and dream of holding my children, but my new pain medication wasn't as sedating as the morphine. I fell asleep easily at first, but every call on the overhead speaker and each nurse who ventured into my room stirred me. Once awake, worry started all over again.

Finally I moved back to the fourth floor, and an entire week of staring at the ceiling wore my patience down. I wanted my life back. I should have been sitting in a wheelchair by now, but I couldn't even do that.

My only joy was seeing my physical therapists every day. They moved my arms, legs, and fingers through Range of Motion exercises to keep my muscles from constricting. They educated me about what to expect in rehab. They spoke of electronic stimulation that could strengthen and maybe stimulate my muscles to move on their own. I wanted desperately to begin, but wondered if it would ever happen.

Just when I thought I would spend the rest of my life in bed, a dear friend and cherished mentor walked into my room. Barb Sellers led the women's weekly Bible study I attended, and every week I sat spellbound as she shared all that God had revealed during her husband's battle with cancer and eventual death two years earlier. Busy at home with teenage children, Barb now ran her late husband's retail store as well. I couldn't imagine her tragic loss and drastic life-change! Yet, in her wisdom, this beautiful, Godly woman mustered the strength and determination to help others with her story of God's provision.

I appreciated Barb's timely visit more than she could have known. She presented me with a deep mahogany plaque donning the words, "God is Faithful," engraved in English script. I nearly cried. Just seeing my friend reminded me of God's faithfulness. Now I had something to bring it to mind long after she left. Mom strategically placed the little keepsake on a stand directly ahead where I could see and believe that God was now writing my story of his faithfulness.

On the heels of Barb's visit, one of my favorite respiratory therapists arrived in time for my next breathing treatment. Jeff was intrigued with my stories of the accident and even added me to his own church's prayer chain.

While I inhaled medicated steam through a blue tube in my mouth, Jeff set a letter-sized sheet of blue parchment paper on my bed tray. My eyes fell to the italicized black words,

> *Even youths grow tired and weary, and young men stumble and fall; but those who hope in the LORD will renew their strength. They will soar on wings like eagles; they will run and not grow weary, they will walk and not be faint.*
> **- ISAIAH 40:30-31**

I was forbidden to speak during my treatments, but Jeff acknowledged the unspoken appreciation glistening in my teary eyes. He smiled and nodded. God wrote this message just for me,

I was sure of it.

My friend reminded me of God's faithfulness through three little words on a wooden plaque, and God immediately reinforced it with His own Word. Some may have called the timing coincidence; I called it providence.

The medical world urged us to wake up to the reality of their experience and accept that recovery was hopeless. But God urged us to hold on to Truth. So we did. We clung to the reality that God is faithful, and healing was possible. He was just getting started.

---

1 *"The Only Hope I Need" written by Phil Morgan. ©1996 Jammin' Gentile Music, BMI. Used by permission. From the Jubalee Music CD "Phil & Pam Morgan - Faith, Hope & Love"*

2 *"God Chooses Who He Uses" written by Phil Morgan. ©1999 Jammin' Gentile Music, BMI. Used by permission. From the Jubalee Music CD "Phil & Pam Morgan - What Matters Most"*

A Flicker of Hope

Now faith is being sure of what we hope
for and certain of what we do not see.

HEBREWS 11:1

"Oooh! Aaah!" rippled through the group as colorful bursts of
fireworks trailed amidst a sparkling night sky backdrop.

A year ago Phil and I celebrated the Fourth of July in the country
with our best friends, stuffing ourselves full of Brenda's home-fried
chicken, corn on the cob, and watermelon. By day we reclined in
lawn chairs beneath a gigantic old oak tree, laughing and letting
our food settle, while the kids blew bubbles through the air and
chased them all over the yard. At twilight we spread blankets in the
field to marvel at the beauty overhead; stars just didn't come that
brilliant or plentiful in the city.

This year the fourth of July marked one month since the wreck.
I was ready to celebrate, and for good reason – my body was on
the mend. The pneumonia was gone, I could swallow again, and
Dr. Schnabel removed the feeding tube from my nose. Finally, I
could drink water in its natural liquid state (not that disgusting
thickened stuff) and eat real food! I could have kissed the menu
planners for serving my favorite dessert – chocolate layer cake –
with my first meal. The cafeteria delivery lady was so amused by

my excitement she snuck me an extra piece! To top it all off, Dr. Schnabel announced I was ready to go, and at the end of the week I would transfer to The Rehabilitation Institute of Kansas City.

I was ecstatic! Until now, it seemed I would never leave the hospital, never see home again, but with Dr. Schnabel's announcement, I could finally detect a glimmer of light at the end of this long, dark tunnel of misery. Hope shone as vividly as the fireworks I remembered, and I could feel it...physically.

My legs ached, a deep and dull ache, similar to what you feel when sitting in a cramped position for hours. I looked forward to my physical therapists' visits. Stretching my legs brought intense relief.

"That feels sooo good...," I moaned as a PT rotated my left foot forward and back, and left to right.

"Can you feel that?" he said.

"Ahhh, yes," I said. "My left leg screams to be moved."

"Really!"

He lifted my leg straight up and guarded my knee. I could tell from his expression he was intrigued.

"That's a good sign, Pam."

Strangely, my legs felt like they could move. In fact, if I closed my eyes, it was hard to convince me they remained still. Some said it was all in my head; my brain simply remembered the sensation of moving. Perhaps. But I wouldn't let their theories destroy my hope.

Dr. Coufal discovered slight sensation in my feet a few days before. Occasionally I could identify when and where he touched. The nurses were amazed – one of them even told Phil I would be their miracle patient.

Now this "good sign" motivated me even more to keep at it. I wanted my feet in plain sight, uncovered, pressed against the foot board of my bed, toes pointed to the sky. Over and over again I tried to make them move.

I'm sure many thought I was in denial, refusing to accept my loss. In part they were right. I did refuse to accept it. Instead, I clung to the truth that God could heal me. I fully realized that

God didn't heal everyone who asked, and I didn't arrogantly think I deserved it more than someone else. I just believed He *could* do it, and felt Him distinctly impressing upon me that He *would*.

God had already spared my life, protected me from brain injury and countless other things that could have happened or gone wrong. He sent encouragement from unexpected places just in the nick of time. I believed God wanted to show the world that He still worked miracles today by performing one in me. Right or wrong, truth or denial, that's what I believed, and whenever I thought about what God had done and what He could do, unexplainable peace settled over me like a warm blanket.

Unfortunately, impatience was a familiar adversary. Regaining sensation was good, but why couldn't I move? The frustrated words of my dad long ago echoed in my memory. Waiting on four teenage daughters to get ready often made him late.

"What's the holdup?" he'd holler.

The same sentiment rattled through my mind these days as I grew more and more restless with God's tardiness. Laying in bed, I would miss too much of life. Something had to change.

Jeff's encouragement from Isaiah hung on the wall. *Those who hope in the LORD will renew their strength…*

Okay, I thought, *I'm hoping…* Every day I watched my feet, remembering how it felt to wiggle my toes, all the while focusing… trying to send the urgent message south.

Our friend and road manager, Barb Underwood, decided to improve the scenery by painting my toenails scarlet red. Not only would the bright color help me focus, she said, my toes would look pretty, too, and it was time to feel better about myself. As my self-proclaimed beautician, Barb pulled a razor, hairbrush, and nail polish from her handy bag of tricks to do the job up right. At first I wasn't very enthusiastic, but once she got started, it felt good to enjoy the superficial indulgences of being a woman again instead of centralizing on mere survival.

With an electric razor, Barb cleared the patchy forest growing up around the grafts and wounds on my long limp legs. When she finished, she shook the bottle of polish until the beads rattled inside.   Twisting the lid open, Barb slid the brush saturated with shiny crimson across the mouth of the jar, releasing the unmistakable odor. For me, it was a refreshing whiff of normalcy, but Phil obviously didn't think so. Slouching in a chair with his feet propped on the edge of my bed, he wrinkled his nose.

"That stuff smells nasty!" he said.

"Oh, hush!" Barb said, "It isn't any worse than all the other smells in this place!"

"She's got a point," I chuckled, amused by the typical banter between Barb and Phil.

Barb is a fun-loving, independent single woman who looks and acts much younger than her golden years. She volunteered to help our ministry wherever we needed her. Barb started manning our product table at local concerts, and gradually moved into traveling with us on weekends to oversee set-up, tear-down and product sales. Her enthusiastic and generous spirit is invaluable. And Barb's tenacious love for the Lord, sprung from a somewhat turbulent past, combines with easy-going humor to make her a delight. Her clever spunk comes in especially handy when pitted against my husband's wit. With Barb and I as teammates, two against one is even-sided.

Barb leaned over my feet to apply the first stroke of red. Unable to see through her arm, I closed my eyes and imagined how it felt to curl my toes.

Suddenly, Barb spun around and squealed.

"Pam! Your toe! It moved!"

"Really?"

"Yes! Do it again! Do it again!"

Phil suddenly summoned a distinct interest in my painted toes. His feet plopped to the floor, and he leaned in for a closer look.

I closed my eyes again to remember my exact instruction, but this time my toe didn't move. Barb froze, nail polish dripping on the floor, her attention fixed on my foot. I opened my eyes and tried again, and again. Nothing.

Still, overwhelming elation broke out in the room, and our praise echoed down the hall! One would have thought I jumped out of bed and walked across the floor. That one little move, no matter how slight, was a sign from heaven that I would indeed walk again. We were all sure of it.

"Thank you, God!" I gasped.

Barb finished her pedicure, giddy with excitement. She practically bounced out of the room when it was time to go, defying the painful arthritis in her knees that usually spoiled her age's secret. Phil reached for his laptop, eager to tell our friends and ministry followers my big news. And I wanted to show everyone, especially the doctors – perhaps now they would share my vision.

My toe performed beautifully over the next couple of days. Family, friends, and nurses all rejoiced with me. But I failed to produce even the slightest quiver for Dr. Patel and Dr. Coufal, who were eager to see what all the hubbub was about.

"I must have performance anxiety," I sighed.

Dr. Coufal chuckled.

"Well, there's always tomorrow," he said.

Dr. Patel explained it could have been a muscle spasm or involuntary twitch, a common side effect of spinal cord injuries.

"No, I don't think so," I said. "I tried to move my toe, and it did!"

"Okay," he said, relenting. "Perhaps the muscle is tired."

I understood what the doctor meant, but it seemed a little funny to me that the muscle could be tired. How could it be tired when all it had been doing for the past three weeks was resting? It should have been full of energy! I longed for it to be, and not only for my benefit. I wanted everyone to know the God I knew. A God who hung the stars in space, who parted the Red Sea, and opened the eyes of the blind. A God who healed the lame… I wanted them to know peace and joy beyond understanding. I wanted them to know Hope, and to see Him in action.

Dr. Schnabel got the opportunity early Saturday morning to see not only a stunning presentation, he got an encore. My right toe arrived on cue with a trace flutter. The smile and surprise on my doctor's face was better than a standing ovation.

Dr. Schnabel was a serious character, yet he revealed tenderness behind the sober professionalism that was endearing to me. Before my last plastic surgery, Dr. Schnabel discussed with Mom and me how long it would take my facial injuries to heal. Mom sighed sadly as she showed the doctor the cover photo on our latest CD.

"She was always such a beautiful girl," she said.

Dr. Schnabel looked at the photo and back at my puffy, wounded face.

"She still looks beautiful to me," he said without hesitation and smiled. From the look on his face, we weren't to argue his expertise. I wondered if he could see a flush of appreciation in my cheeks amidst the bandages.

First and foremost, Dr. Schnabel's job was to save lives. I believe he did it so well because of how much he cared for his patients. He had directed and overseen my condition and treatment closely every day for the past three weeks. I watched the vigilant care he extended. Dr. Schnabel rarely took a day off (which I chastised him for repeatedly), but he never seemed to tire of his work. Graciously he answered our never-ending questions day in and day out, always straightforward, but never abrupt.

In the wake of this exciting turn of events, my doctor was careful to applaud, but not overly encourage.

"I'm going to walk back in here to see you someday, you know," I said.

Dr. Schnabel diplomatically avoided comment, yet his eyes told all.

"I don't think so," they said.

The doctor wasn't willing to go that far. Granted, slight toe movement is a far cry from walking across the room. And yet, it was a complete surprise in his world of medicine. For me, it was confirmation, a flicker of hope, and while Dr. Schnabel had his doubts, he respected my determination with a nod.

Dr. Schnabel scribbled in my chart. "Moved toes today! Left more than right!" His use of exclamation marks could have simply expressed how pleased he was, but I believed they inscribed much more.

Over the next few days I continued to perpetuate medical

confusion as I began to slightly rock my knee back and forth. The change in atmosphere was fun to watch, like an unexpected upset in a football game. Suddenly the underdog had the ball, and took off running toward the end zone. Sympathetic staff attitudes turned to eager anticipation. Nurses, technicians, and therapists became my cheerleaders, excited to see what would happen next. One nurse boldly said, "I have read the chart...she is a miracle."

Dr. Coufal didn't use those precise words, but his candid perception of the situation exuded fascination.

"This isn't something I expected, Pam," he said. "This is the first time I have ever reversed a prognosis."

"What do you mean exactly by reverse prognosis?"

"All the doctors who examined you diagnosed your injury as complete," he said.

"Complete?"

Dr. Coufal explained complete versus incomplete injuries – a complete injury offers no chance for recovery. Period.

"Pam, you were a complete injury," he said emphatically.

"And now?"

"You're as incomplete as they come," he said, still bemused.

Phil grinned sheepishly. His eyes met mine, and instantly, I knew my husband's thoughts were the same as mine. This was huge. Hope and excitement intensified as I listened to the expert officially explain my original prognosis and watched his amazement. If Dr. Coufal was surprised now, I couldn't wait to see his reaction when God healed me completely.

I started to blurt my convictions, but then hesitated. What would he think? Would he silence my enthusiasm by labeling me an unrealistic fanatic? Dr. Coufal sensed my hesitation and paused, encouraging me to speak. I decided to take the chance.

"You know, what is happening here is way beyond any of us," I said. "You are a tool in my healing, but God is ultimately the one in control."

Dr. Coufal smiled, but didn't say a word. Perhaps he thought I was crazy, it was hard to tell; and yet, he didn't dismiss the idea.

Independence Day seemed so fitting...the perfect holiday to

celebrate, I thought. In rehab I would soon regain my independence, go home to my family, and the world would recognize God's power and faithfulness.

Yet wiggling a toe or rotating a knee wasn't enough to get me out of bed and back into life. As the sun set, impatience reared its ugly head once again, and my zeal quickly fizzled away, just like the pathetic excuse for fireworks outside my window.

Phil spent the evening having fun and making new memories with the girls somewhere in town. Even the usual nursing staff had taken the night off to celebrate. Meanwhile, Mom and I spent the evening with a grumpy fill-in nurse, eating snack cups of sherbet and trying to catch an occasional glimpse of a wimpy spark around the brick wall that blocked our view.

I was perturbed. I remembered last year's fun and depression returned. A precious opportunity to make new and exciting holiday memories with my young daughters had been stolen. I looked at Barb's gift plaque and then at the words from Isaiah hanging on my wall, searching for consolation. They gave me peace for the long haul, but at the moment, they didn't help at all. I wanted to soar, run, or at the very least, walk and join my family right *now*. Nothing else mattered. I just wanted to go home.

The Hardest Part

…Come and listen, all you who fear God;
let me tell you what he has done for me…

PSALMS 66:16

"Got 10 minutes? Sit down – have I got a story to tell you!"

Daily I beckoned nurses, aids, therapists, and janitors to listen to what had happened to me. I eagerly boasted about how God had spared my life to anyone and everyone who entered my room. Most were incredibly gracious, like my young therapist on the morning of my departure, who was captivated and amazed at what God had done.

"You have been the topic of conversation in our floor meetings and in the break room," she said. "I know I'm not your regular therapist, but I asked to see you again today. After working with you yesterday and listening to your story, I just had to come again."

I loved these precious people. I was convinced that God had hand-picked each one to be blessed and bless me in return. Like Simonle, the Catholic hospital chaplain, who visited me faithfully even though I wasn't Catholic. When he heard I was leaving, Simonle presented me with a scarlet rose as a token of his appreciation. The kind and gentle young man said after visiting with our family and watching our faith, God told him it was time to get serious about his own Christian walk.

Betty was a boldly charismatic nurse's aid, who was determined God would work a miracle of healing in me. Not usually assigned to my floor, Betty and I met when she filled in for someone on vacation. From then on, she visited me on coffee breaks and even on her days off to pray healing over my body. She often brought a friend along to hear my story and join her in prayer. My Missouri Synod Lutheran mother was often caught a little off guard by her boisterous animation, and yet Betty's voice of faith was invigorating and incredibly encouraging.

Then there was Dr. Patel's assistant, Annetta. Her bubbly compassion set me at ease from the very beginning. She wanted to see me walk again almost as much as I did. Annetta was fun to be around, and I became one of her favorite patients. She hated to see me go somewhere else for therapy, but in light of my situation, she admitted that a highly-ranked facility specializing in spinal cord injuries was the best place for me.

The morning I was to leave, Annetta dropped in to say goodbye. To be honest, I felt a little nervous about the move, and Annetta encouraged me as she held a chilling contrast of before and after x-rays up to the light. Screws and plates now straightened my neck securely in its proper position.

"The fusion looks great and is healing quickly!" she said.

"Good," I said. "Can I take this annoying brace off?"

"Not yet, little missy! Give it another month. In the meantime, let's get you home!"

"I'm going home?" My heart leaped at the thought.

"Eventually," she said. "After a few weeks at the Institute, you should be ready."

"How many weeks?"

"Not less than two, but probably no more than four."

"Oh, that's not so bad," I said.

Annetta set the x-rays down and rested her hand on my leg, her expression suddenly serious.

"The hardest part is yet to come," she said. "Rehab is slow and grueling, and won't end when you go home. The entire process can take up to two years."

"That's OK," I said, "What else have I got to do?"

My flippant response amused Annetta, but also revealed my naiveté. I couldn't begin to understand the truth in her words. I had no idea what the "entire process" entailed.

At 11:00 am the ambulance arrived to transport me uptown. Annetta held my hand as the EMT wheeled my gurney to the elevator. She leaned in and kissed me on the cheek, and I noticed a moist glisten in her eyes.

"I'm gonna miss you," Annetta whispered, and quickly turned to leave so that I wouldn't see her emotion.

As the doors opened, dread loomed over me. A new place with people I didn't know – and who didn't know me – awaited. Annetta's words echoed in my mind as I watched her retreat down the hallway, *The hardest part is yet to come...*

chapter nine

Get to the "9"

Give your entire attention to what God is
doing right now, and don't get worked up
about what may or may not happen tomorrow.
God will help you deal with whatever hard
things come up when the time comes.
MATTHEW 6:34 (MSG)

I'd forgotten the brilliant blue of a morning sky and the whispering swish of summer leaves in the wind. It seemed like forever since I had been outdoors. The warm July breeze brushed my face, and what senses I still possessed were overwhelmed. I could have stayed outside for hours, but I was only allowed to relish a few brief minutes before the EMTs lifted my gurney into the ambulance, and anchored it to the floor. I scanned the interior and cringed slightly to think of the last time I was in one of these things.

No, I thought. *Enjoy the ride. Enjoy the outdoors.*

I soon discovered that would be hard to do. As we pulled out of the parking lot, memories of my first roller coaster experience came rushing back. And so did the old familiar queasiness. Each jostle, bump, turn, start, and stop lunged my limp body against the straps that held me hostage. I shifted my gaze outside, hunting for something to distract me. I tried focusing on the crisp outline of puffy clouds against the turquoise sky and the ornate stonework of old buildings along the boulevard, yet each slight turn took my breath away. I was relieved when we finally pulled into the circle drive of the Rehabilitation Institute. I used to hurry to get back in line when the roller coaster came to a stop so I could do it all over again. Not now. I was glad this ride was over. Or was it?

Rolling through the automatic sliding doors, I heard a deep, syrupy-sweet male voice.

"Who is *this* beautiful creature?"

I would typically suspect such an obviously mistaken sugar-coated observation, but not with this man. Leonard, the receptionist, somewhat resembled a teddy-bear with his short white receding hair, round nose, and surprisingly genuine, warm smile. Without warning I blushed, and a huge smile spread across my face in return. He honestly thought I was stunning! Or so he had me convinced. Ha! Someone needed to check his vision.

"Pam Morgan, transfer from Research Medical Center," one of the EMTs said.

"Welcome, Pam," Leonard said, dripping with enthusiasm. "It is wonderful to have you!"

Leonard was charming, and a favorite among the patients, male and female alike. Such sincerity and heartfelt affirmation seemed a bit over the top, yet it was exactly the welcome I needed.

When the elevator doors opened on the second floor, I took inventory of the new surroundings. The nurse's station lay directly across the hall. On the wall behind, a huge whiteboard printed each patient's name and room in black, doctor in red, and weekly schedule in blue. I found my name. "Morgan, Room 210, Berger."

We turned left out of the elevator, and then left again. About twenty feet down the hall, we stopped at a wide doorway on the right. "Room 210," the sign read.

It actually looked homey, almost like a real bedroom. A coordinating swirl border topped the pastel-textured wallpaper. To my left, the open bathroom door exposed a handicapped accessible toilet and sink. Next to the door, a television suspended from the ceiling, and beneath it, a square daily calendar with the day's date in large type hung on the wall across from the bed.

A nurse followed me in to take my vitals and ask questions, recording my answers on a clipboard. When she finished her admittance report, she asked what I ate for lunch.

"Nothing. I left before lunch was served."

"Oh," she said, looking at her watch. "Well, the cafeteria is closed, but I'll check to see what I can do."

I wasn't very hungry, but eating would pass the time. They must have had leftovers, because in a little while, she brought a tray and set it down in front of me on the stand over my bed. Then she turned to leave. I was dumbfounded. Couldn't she see that I was alone? Phil and Mom had stayed behind to pack my things at the hospital, and hadn't arrived yet.

"Umm, excuse me," I called after her. "I can't feed myself."

Again she looked at her watch. I got the impression she had other things to do.

"I thought someone would have helped you with that by now," she said. "We don't normally feed the patients."

She was pleasant and didn't mean to be cruel, but at the time, her comment seemed rather inappropriate. In the hospital, the nurses did everything for me or made sure someone was there to help. Obviously that wouldn't be the case here.

"Is it even possible for me to do that? I mean, my fingers don't work at all. I can't hold anything."

"Honey, you will be amazed what lies in the realm of possibility," she said and offered a spoonful of mashed potatoes and gravy.

———❧———

By mid-afternoon Phil and Mom had arrived after grabbing a bite of lunch at a neighborhood fast food place. I reclined in bed staring out the window as they busily unpacked my things. Dense pear-shaped foliage of Bradford Pear trees swayed and sparkled in the wind amidst peaks and dormers of a beautiful residential neighborhood. I soaked in the gorgeous view that looked so much like home and thought of my girls. My heart ached.

Phil strategically hung pictures of the girls next to the calendar and taped Kayla's love notes and artwork that she proudly prepared for me on the wall beside my bed. My favorite was a crayon masterpiece of the two of us holding hands.

Everything was perfectly placed when a thin brown-haired man knocked on the frame around my open door. He didn't wait for a response; he just let himself in. Looking more like an eccentric college professor than a medical doctor, this man was quite a change in character from Dr. Schnabel. He wore a casual button-down shirt, knit tie, and cotton twill trousers, and his brown straight hair flopped loosely across his forehead.

Dr. Gary Berger introduced himself. He was forward and genuinely pleasant, but there was a quirkiness about him I couldn't quite put my finger on.

In a whirlwind monologue, Dr. Berger gave me a run-down of what to expect over the next several weeks. An abbreviated therapy schedule ensued on the weekends – thirty minutes each of physical and occupational therapy – with the full regimen beginning Monday morning.

"I have selected Shannon Lepper and Cathie DeVries for your physical and occupational therapists respectively," he said, "You won't find any better."

"You may want to ward off visitors for a few days," he said as a side note, "You will be exhausted."

Dr. Berger pulled my covers back to begin a thorough physical exam, revealing my lovely hospital gown.

"Street clothes and pajamas from now on!"

"Oh, hallelujah!" I said.

"Just make them comfortable and easy to get on and off," he said, and turned to address Mom and Phil. "Button-up shirts, elastic waists...that kind of thing."

He pulled my gown and bandage from my left shoulder and peered over his glasses. The wound had soaked through the dressing.

"By the looks of things, you may want to wear something you don't mind getting dirty," he said and pushed the call button for a nurse, "I'll have someone change this for you."

"Sweats are best. Absolutely no jeans."

He walked around to the foot of my bed and examined my feet, rotating them at the ankles.

"And you will need high top tennis shoes for support," he deduced, adding, "To avoid foot-drop, I'll order a pair of PRAFOs for you to wear in bed."

PRAFOs looked something like ski boots. Their sole purpose (no pun intended) was to hold my feet perpendicular to my legs while in bed to keep my Achilles tendon from shortening.

Mom jotted a shopping list.

"First thing we need to do is remove the Foley catheter," Dr. Berger said, and without further warning, the doctor gently and swiftly removed it.

"But then, how will I go to the bathroom?" I asked.

"You will need to be catheterized every four to six hours."

"For how long?"

"Indefinitely," he said.

Dr. Berger saw the shock on my face and sensed I didn't fully understand the permanence of my condition. His expression sobered as he looked me square in the eye.

"You must realize there is no cure for spinal cord injuries."

Annetta's departing words again echoed in my mind, but now they were trumped by what I just heard. Her "two year" prediction turned into forever. I wanted to like this man, but I really hated what he just said and did so suddenly. I mulled over what "intermittent cathing" meant for my privacy and dignity over the rest of my life. From now on, someone else would routinely drain my bladder through a little plastic tube.

"Smile for me," Dr. Berger said.

His command caught me completely off-guard. I didn't feel like smiling; I was still trying to process all of this. And yet, I couldn't help it. I felt lured into a trap.

"Ah, what a great smile!" he beamed, "I look forward to seeing that everyday."

He lingered only a brief second before snapping back to reality. The clock was ticking and he had a schedule to keep.

"Until tomorrow..." he popped with a quick salute, and as quickly as he arrived, he was gone.

My smile disappeared instantaneously. This was a scary new place, and I wasn't sure what to think or how I'd make it over the next several weeks.

Fortunately, Dee set me at ease. Upon meeting the head floor nurse, it was obvious they had chosen the right person to be in charge. All the nurses and techs reported to Dee. She reminded me of a mother hen – kind, caring, and protective, yet tight in enforcing the rules. She kept her coop in order. Her spunk was not about to let anyone supersede her authority. Yet, tenderness radiated from her, and I felt confident that I would be in good hands when Dee was around.

"The most important thing to remember is that you are in charge of directing your care," she said.

Phil's glance said he didn't understand what that meant any more than I did, but we both nodded and chose to file it away for another time. We were both tired.

Phil and Mom still planned to stay with me alternating days. A few days earlier the general manager tried to tell me the rules of this facility didn't allow family members to spend the night as I had grown accustomed. She didn't get very far before I emphatically insisted this rule be broken. In essence I said that if rehab was as difficult as everyone said, I would need the support and presence of my family more than ever. After all, I didn't live alone before, and I would be going home to live with my family again, so it was cruel to take them away when I needed them most. In all honesty, I felt like an insecure, scared little girl, and I couldn't face being alone.

Whatever I said, I must have sounded convincing, because she conceded to make an exception. She even agreed to give me a private room. Each was designed for double occupancy, but she allowed a family member to sleep in the other bed as long as the facility didn't fill to capacity.

Phil stayed with me the first night. Mom arrived early the next morning carrying a white plastic bag full of new purchases, as well as some clothes and pajamas from home. This first glimpse of normalcy was exciting, and Mom and I began to chatter about her shopping excursion the day before. Phil decided it was time to go.

My heart sank into a pit in my stomach, and tears rolled down my cheeks. I didn't want him to leave, at least not so soon. My first full day in this new world lay before me, and I wanted my husband with me. I needed my his light-hearted, everything-is-gonna-be-OK attitude, his jokes and witty comments, his way of knowing what I needed without me saying a word, his kiss, his touch.

"Hey, look," Phil said tenderly, pointing to the wall calendar. A big, bold "8" stared back at me.

"All you have to do is focus on getting to the '9'. That's it. That's all you have to do. One day. Just get to the '9'. Got it?"

I nodded and squeezed my eyes shut to try and stop the tears. I had to let him go. Kayla and Alisha waited eagerly for Daddy at home. I was their mom; I should have wanted him to go. Why then, did I feel like the child?

Phil stayed a few more minutes until I could keep from falling apart as he neared the door. He kissed me and promised to return early the next day.

As Phil walked out, his words stayed with me, and I glanced at the calendar once more.

chapter ten

Facing the Facts

Search me, O God, and know my heart;
test me and know my anxious thoughts.

PSALMS 139:23

A soft-spoken nurse's aid named Stephanie rolled me from side to side, inching my navy blue sweats up and over my hips. My first therapy session was scheduled at 9:00 a.m., so she pulled my gray baseball shirt over my shoulders, buttoned it up, and wedged my sock-clad feet into stiff, new sparkling-white high-tops.

My feet hadn't seen shoes in over a month, and they hung like lead weights from the bed as Stephanie swung me into position for transferring. The nurse's aide was quiet and sweet-spirited, and built from solid stock. Her strength amazed me as she effortlessly hoisted me into the wheelchair.

"Wow! That was easy," I said.

"Just the way it's supposed to be," she said.

Stephanie possessed a sincere desire to help her patients feel comfortable and secure. Already I knew she would be one of my favorites.

"Do you want me to take you to the sink?"

"Please," I said.

Stephanie situated me in front of the mirror above the bathroom sink. I had hoped fresh clothes would improve what I saw a few days before.

Back at the hospital, Phil had offered a mirror during a bandage change. I hadn't remembered seeing myself at all and hadn't given much thought to my appearance under the circumstances. My friends and family were good at concealing the truth about my horrific appearance.

At first I declined taking a look, comfortable in my ignorance. But I reconsidered. I needed to see it. I needed to know the truth.

"OK, let me see..."

Phil held the mirror, and I closed my eyes to muster the courage to peek. Opening one eye and then the other, I peered at the person looking back at me. I felt numb -- and a bit relieved to see that I still looked like me. A torn, bruised and battered me, but me nonetheless.

With Phil as my tour guide, I surveyed the damage. Both eyebrows were beginning to grow back. Skin resembling fish scales pulled across my outer eyebrow and down my temple just missing my eye. The new silvery patch from my scalp was full of holes where hair had once poked through. I wondered if they would ever go away.

Shifting focus to my hair, I winced at my greasy bed head. Two weeks and one plastic surgery since the nurse washed my hair, wound salve and yellow gauze still clung like glue to the top of my head. Barb had worked tediously to clear much of the dried blood and tangles, but a few chunks hung on stubbornly here and there.

Phil rotated the mirror slightly to reflect my left ear, still peppered with dried blood. A fresh incision tucked skillfully into the vertical crease in front just above my jaw line. Back to the right, Phil pointed out the large pink wound puncturing the side of my nose. Then he focused my attention on stitches stretched across an open gash in the center of my forehead.

"That one was the size of a silver dollar," he said, concluding the Tour of Wounds, "Doc didn't think it would close as well as it has."

Hmmm. "Well" was certainly a matter of opinion. I wasn't sure if I agreed with my doctor just yet.

Now as I prepared for my first therapy session and stared again at my reflection over the sink, I was disappointed. I looked ugly and awkward in my bulky bandages, neck collar, and loose clothing now way too big for my atrophied body. Acne plagued my forehead; stress and medication were too much for my skin to handle. I felt like a self-conscious, apprehensive teenager on the first day of gym class.

"Ugh!" I gasped.

"Aw, you look beautiful," Stephanie said.

I wished. Just prior to the accident, I had lost 40 pounds and was working out regularly, feeling better than ever. I was an active wife and mother with a tender-hearted daughter about to start Kindergarten and a curious dimple-faced little girl toddling about. Wheelchairs and a struggling self-image did not fit into my life. Nevertheless, here I sat, a limp lump of skin and bones covered with ugly flesh wounds.

Just as I began to throw myself into a decent sulk, Jeanette, the head of therapy, showed up to wheel me down to therapy. The large open gym was filled with exercise equipment galore and bright blue therapy mats atop wooden frames. A variety of wheelchairs sat vacant in the corner. All was quiet, except for a stunning young woman zooming around the room's perimeter in her little black sport wheelchair. In stark contrast to my awkward, sloppy appearance, the petite blonde wore coordinated workout attire and wielded weights with incredible strength. She was obviously not a patient here, and this was certainly not her first day.

This energetic dynamo captured my whole attention. I saw her stretch and reach above her head, pull a towel down and wipe the sweat. For many, an unimpressive move. For me...phenomenal! Her strength and agility was mesmerizing. She was completely self-sufficient. No one pushed her, held things for her, or wiped her face.

"Ce, how good to see you!" Jeanette said. "What brings you in on a Saturday?"

"I have a date for a dinner party coming up."

Ce lifted barbells into place.

"My little black dress...needs to fit...," she said, pumping bicep curls.

Here was a refined, muscular woman, not much older than me, in a wheelchair. She had been selected for a date...in a wheelchair. I was dumbfounded. Not because someone found her attractive, but because life was so normal for her...in a wheelchair.

I could have watched Ce all day. She made disability look easy. I wanted to know her story – every spinal cord injury patient has one to tell. Evidently, some time had passed since her injury. How did she get to this point?

Another young woman approached me.

"Hi, Pam, I'm Shannon. I'll be your physical therapist," she said pleasantly and sat on the edge of the mat.

"We'll start with an initial evaluation, but before we begin, I have a question for you."

Shannon grabbed her clipboard and pen.

"What is your goal for therapy?"

That was simple.

"To leave here without the wheelchair," I said confidently. What else would it be?

Shannon didn't say a word. She just nodded and wrote down my answer. She wasn't surprised, I later discovered. Most of her patients say the same thing.

"OK, then, let's get you over here on the mat."

"Just so you know," I said, "don't touch my shoulder!"

Shannon maneuvered the wheelchair adjacent to the mat's edge and examined my wounds. She removed the arm of the chair, leaving a clear path for smooth transferring. Shannon grabbed the gait belt draped over her shoulder and fastened it around my waist. Then with the same ease and vigor as Stephanie, she lifted and swung my rear to the mat.

"Use your arms to stabilize yourself," she said.

"Don't let go!" I cried in fear.

"I won't, I won't...I've got you!"

Shannon held my body steady and sat down directly in front of me on a rolling stool. Her legs straddled mine and she held me upright supporting my good shoulder.

"Can you find your center of balance?" she said, instructing again, "Use your arms like a tripod."

I couldn't. It was bizarre. I felt like a rag doll with no concept of where my body was in space. I couldn't feel anything in my torso from my shoulders down, so if I closed my eyes, I couldn't tell where I was in relation to the mat or the ground.

I grunted and strained to try and hold myself upright as Shannon instructed. She attempted to release her grip, and I was terrified by the realization that the trifle of strength I had left in my arms wasn't enough to do the job. I felt I would most definitely topple forward into a heap on the floor, or into Shannon's lap, one of the two. My head began to swim.

"I'm getting dizzy..." I gasped, short of breath.

Shannon strengthened her grip and gently eased my body back against a monstrous foam wedge covered in blue vinyl. I wanted to cry.

"Rest for a few minutes, and we'll try again," Shannon soothed.

Breathing heavily, I gazed at Ce busily continuing her workout in the background. Shannon noticed how I watched her, and most likely, sensed my envy.

"Ce, come over here a minute," she said. "There's someone I'd like you to meet.

Shannon introduced us, and Ce and I swapped stories. Ce willingly shared that she, too, was also thrown from her vehicle as it crashed nearly twenty years earlier. Fortunately, she landed on grass, so her flesh injuries were minor in comparison. Yet she remembered all too well the pain and struggle of her early days of paralysis. Ce graciously answered my questions and confessed her current challenges.

I was fascinated. Although her legs were motionless, she was trim and seemed to support herself easily in the armless chair.

"Look at you now," I said, "You are so thin, and you have full use of your abdominal muscles."

Ce shook her head.

"Uh-uh, it's an illusion," she said, "It's all arms and shoulders, and I have to watch what I eat..."

Amazing. Ce was a pro at compensating, using her arms and shoulders to maintain balance, posture, and function. She was graceful...and beautiful.

I thought again about my goal for rehab. Maybe I was fooling myself. I had so far to go... perhaps too far.

After two more tries it became evident that sitting independently was not meant to be, at least not for that day. Shannon gave in, and let me rest flat on the mat to see if I could move any part of my legs or feet voluntarily. I had boasted proudly about my toes and knee, and she was eager to check them out. But my toes wouldn't cooperate.

Shannon wrote, "strength absent, except for *trace* left hip abduction."

I was devastated.

Upon each assessment, I required the maximum assistance possible to sit, lie down, roll over, transfer... I was completely dependent.

Shannon concluded her evaluation with a new set of rehab goals, quite a bit different from my own.

> *1. Patient/Family will demonstrate*
> *understanding of education provided.*
> *2. Patient will maintain sitting at edge of mat*
> *without upper extremity support.*
> *3. Patient will perform bed mobility and*
> *transfers with moderate assist.*

That was it. No walking, not even with assistance.

"You will make progress and build endurance, but it'll be slow," Shannon said firmly, yet gently.

I nodded in understanding.

"You're going to need therapy for a long time. We'll do our best to strengthen whatever muscles return, but we can only work with what you have."

I liked Shannon. Dr. Berger did well to pair us together. She was about my age, strong, upbeat, tender-hearted, and gentle. And with a husband and young daughter of her own, she could empathize with my urgent desire to recover and go home. Yet Shannon made the facts perfectly clear. My definition of progress needed to change. Rehab was not a magical place to bring paralyzed muscles back to life. It was simply a place to strengthen those that did work, and teach me how to live with the rest. Just like my appearance, that fact wasn't easy to face.

A Mother's Heart

A mother's love for her child is like
nothing else in the world. It knows no law,
no pity, it dares all things and crushes down
remorselessly all that stands in its path.
AGATHA CHRISTIE

"Come with me!" I cried, frightened and anxious about the moments ahead.

A nurse's aide with a chip the size of Mount Everest on her shoulder wheeled me into the hall.

"You aren't going anywhere without me!" Mom's adamant words were intended not only to soothe my fear, but also to warn the tall, slender woman that her mistreatment better not continue.

Shortly after dinner that evening, the aid came in to prep me for my shower. She was pretty, except for the scowl on her face. She removed my clothes and bandages, and changed my soft neck collar to a hard plastic brace.

I tried to strike up a conversation. Getting to know my caregivers personally seemed to restore some semblance of my dignity and served as a means of distraction. That's when it became apparent this woman didn't like her job very much, and she didn't care for me at all. She didn't want to speak. Instead, she seemed perturbed that I was interrupting the job she had to do. And that's what I was to her...a job.

The aide answered my questions with a curt "yes," "no," or "I don't know." Otherwise, silence. No return questions about me, my life, nothing. In fact, she didn't even ask things that would have been relevant to the task at hand, like "Where does it hurt?" or "Are you comfortable?" Nothing. But she found out the hard way...

Before transferring me to the waterproof shower bed, the aide sat me upright and swung my legs over the side of the bed in such a rough and abrupt way that I nearly slid to the floor. She grabbed my wounded shoulder, and I cried out in intense pain. She sighed and rolled her eyes in annoyance. My head began to spin and my stomach turn. Mom stood by in shock, not knowing what to do or how to help that wouldn't hurt me further.

"Press the call button!" the aide rudely commanded my mother.

Horrified, Mom quickly obliged and the woman summoned help. By the time two or three other women rushed in to assist, I was shaking from fear, pain, and cold. They positioned my bare body on the flat plastic rolling bed, and covered me with a skimpy towel. Tears streamed from my eyes and into my ears. I was completely at the mercy of someone who couldn't care less.

Mom followed us down the hall to the shower room, keeping her promise that I wouldn't go through this alone. The shower continued to be a miserable experience. But at least the aide put forth a little more care with my mother hovering close by.

The head nurse's ambiguous statement about directing my own care when I first arrived was now becoming clear. Once the nightmare ended, I lay bandaged and dressed, shivering under mounds of blankets. Showers were given routinely every other night. I couldn't handle another experience like this one, of that I was sure.

Mom called Phil and held the phone to my ear. I cried again, rehashing the entire frightening experience. The security of Phil's voice was comforting. He insisted we call for Dee.

Of course! Dee – Mother Hen. Mom hung up the phone and pressed the call button again, this time knowing exactly what to do. She was determined I wouldn't be handled that way again. If I didn't make sure of it, she would.

Dee heard our complaints with an apologetic ear.

"In directing my own care," I summarized, "I want to make sure that tonight's aide is never assigned to me again. Can I do that?"

Dee smiled sympathetically and patted my leg.

"I'll see what I can do."

Mom and I breathed a sigh of relief. From the look on Dee's face, we knew it was as good as done.

Ready to call it a night, Mom propped me with pillows and tucked blankets around my body until I resembled a cocoon. She hesitated for a few minutes before turning out the lights. Chatting a little longer allowed lingering emotions to vent and nerves to settle...for both of us. Mom stroked my hair. I prayed aloud, thanking God she was there.

A mother is the truest friend we have, when trials heavy and sudden, fall upon us; when adversity takes the place of prosperity; when friends who rejoice with us in our sunshine desert us; when trouble thickens around us, still will she cling to us, and endeavor by her kind precepts and counsels to dissipate the clouds of darkness, and cause peace to return to our hearts.
- WASHINGTON IRVING

I thought my mom's whole purpose was to be my mom. That's how she made me feel.
- NATASHA GREGSON WAGNER

As a child, I was a clingy mama's baby, a babysitter's nightmare. I didn't let Mom go anywhere without crying and wailing until she returned home. On one hand, Mom admits she was to blame. My parents rarely went out socially – much to Dad's dismay I'm sure. No dinner parties, no theater or movie dates, no romantic weekend get-aways. In fact, I don't remember Mom going anywhere much that she couldn't take me along, probably to spare the sitter as much as to pacify me. I was thirteen before I would finally spend the night at a friend's house without calling Mom in the middle of the night to take me home (which she did every time).

On the other hand, I never doubted Mom's love. She never begrudged me for not having the freedom to do as she wished. Maybe she felt burdened, but I never knew it.

Even as a teenager struggling for independence, I felt completely safe to pour out my thoughts and dreams to mom's patient listening ear. Ideas about faith, boys, parties...she didn't always agree with me, and at times, mom spoiled my fun as she set her wise size-nine foot down on my crazy, naïve plans. Yet she always made time for me – her gentle smile and tender embrace ready to comfort, encourage, or praise. Even Mom's rebukes and discipline reflected her devotion. She loved me too much to let me do something stupid or get away with it if I already had.

I adored my mama and hugged her all the time. She loved my affection and readily returned it, always eager to love me unconditionally.

My sisters echo her praise, and our admiration has deepened as we have become mothers ourselves. Yet our admiration has not come without a hefty price. Mom has cried oceans of tears over her past fifty-plus years of motherhood. The morning before Denise passed away, Sherry and I remember Mom sliding her arm underneath Denise's shoulders in the wee hours. She cradled her eldest daughter in her arms, rocking her back and forth in bed, not only to ease Denise's pain, but also to soothe her own ache of their impending separation.

"Do you remember when you were a little girl and I used to do this?" Mom comforted.

Denise managed to nod slightly. The entire family had gathered and was strewn across the house, sleeping wherever they could find room to stretch out. From our spot near Denise's hospital bed in the family room, Sherry and I tearfully watched Mom's tenderness with her dying daughter. My own Kayla was two and a half at the time. I couldn't imagine Mom's pain. Actually I could, but I didn't want to go there. To think of losing my sweet little girl...

Yes, Mom has paid dearly indeed, and as she stood beside my bed this time, she suffered again.

"I wish I could take your place," Mom said, holding my limp fingers gently in her strong hand. "I keep telling myself that I should be the one in that bed."

"No, Mom," I said, and mused, "then I would have to take care of you."

Mom smiled, yet the worry lines remained in her face. I understood. I understood the maternal instinct to want to shield your young from suffering. If anyone had to get hurt in the accident, I was glad it was me. Still, I ached for my mama, for all she had endured the last three years – losing a daughter and a grandson – and now facing the burden of spending half her time caring for a paralyzed daughter. I felt sorry for Dad as well, especially having to do without Mom all that time.

"Don't worry about it," Daddy would say and smile with a mischievous twinkle in his eye. "If she was at home, she'd just wish she was here, and then she wouldn't be of any use to me at all."

Daddy described the truth of the old proverb, "a mother's heart is always with her children." Oh, how I could relate! Mothers long to be with their children no matter how old they are. And there is something especially intense about the need to hold them close when they are little. The most excruciating pain by far was being separated from my babies day in and day out.

I was overjoyed the next morning when Phil arrived bright and early (just as promised) with a timely surprise. He didn't come alone; Kayla scooted in right beside him. My face lit up like a Christmas tree.

"Mommy!"

Kayla skipped over to me and then stopped short at my bedside as if an invisible wall separated us. For an instant I forgot about my bandages, but as soon as she hesitated, I remembered.

"It's OK," I said, "crawl up here carefully."

Madalene followed behind, carrying Alisha.

"Hey Sweetheart," I cooed. "How's my punkin? I've missed you."

My littlest stared at me timidly, clinging to Grandma's neck, completely comfortable to keep her distance.

I felt that my heart would explode. I wanted to throw my arms around them and hold them so close I could feel their hearts beating.

"It is so good to see you! I've missed you so much!"

Kayla sat on the bed beside my hip with her feet dangling off the edge. I stroked her silky hair with the back of my hand, feeling the softness over my thumb and index finger. She was a little piece of heaven, and she smelled *so* good, just as I remembered.

Alisha glared at me.

"Who is that?" Grandma said, "Who is that over there?"

Alisha pointed at me with a blank expression.

"Is that Mommy?" Grandma hinted.

Alisha nodded her tousled-haired head, still glaring. She wore a cotton sundress I had never seen before. The white bodice hosted an embroidered watermelon slice and gave way to a pink checkered seersucker skirt and matching diaper cover. I continued to sweet-talk Alisha to entice her to come near me. I hoped she would be soothed by my voice even if she didn't recognize me.

No such luck. My used-to-be "Mama's girl" remained uncharacteristically cool and bashful. Alisha got down and explored the room and hallway a little, making a point not to wander close to the bed. Outside the safety of Grandma's arms, she wouldn't even look at me.

To keep my heartache at bay, I focused on Kayla instead, reasoning to myself that Alisha's response was completely natural, and that all would be better when I went home. *What if it wasn't?* cowered in the back of my mind, but I pretended to ignore it.

Meanwhile Kayla chattered about her latest excursion to a friend's house from church. Frequently several helped Madalene by taking the girls for an afternoon. Occasionally, Kayla would briefly interrupt her story with a question of "What's this Mommy?" or "Why do you have this [bandage] on?"

I wanted to soak her into my senses for safe-keeping so that I could recall her essence throughout the day – the sound of her voice, her sweet little face, her soft kiss against my cheek. I tried to fill the void of Alisha's rejection with Kayla's eager affection.

Yet all too soon the patch on the cavern in my heart was ripped away once again. It was time for them to go. A severing pain sliced through me as my own flesh and blood walked out of the room.

As tears flooded my eyes, Mom took my hand. A knowing tear cascaded down her cheek. My mother's heart understood.

> *A mother holds her children's hands for a while…*
> *their hearts forever.*
>
> **- UNKNOWN**

Young love in bloom! Left, Phil and I at my senior prom 1986 and below, four years later at our wedding, October 20, 1990.

Good times, great friends! Our RELIEF accountability group, Joe & Cindy Moses above, and to the right, Alan & Brenda Black, Dave & Allyson Cook, yours truly, and Jamie & Amy Jones.

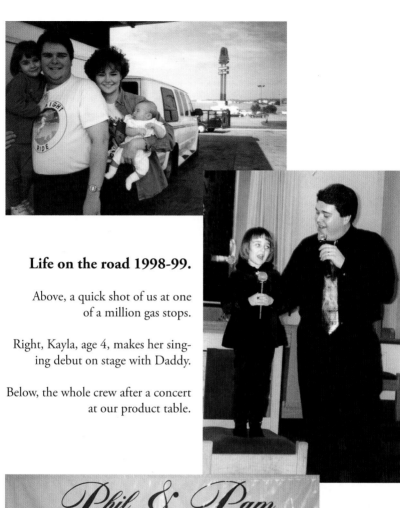

Life on the road 1998-99.

Above, a quick shot of us at one of a million gas stops.

Right, Kayla, age 4, makes her singing debut on stage with Daddy.

Below, the whole crew after a concert at our product table.

Mommy and her babies.

Above left, Kayla flying kites in the park on her fifth birthday.

Above right, Alisha and Mommy take a stroll in Austin, Texas-March 2000.

Below, the last shot of our family together before the accident.
Five days later, everything would change.

Our trusty van has seen better days. I flew through the far back window on the driver's side shown here.

Early ICU photos.

Right, resting peacefully under morphine's trance.

Left, my battered and swollen knees.

Right, posing for the camera during one of my dreaded breathing treatments.

Rebuilding my face.

Right, Dr. Cannova had his work cut out for him. The lower part of my cheek and ear had been reattached. Next would come a series of skin grafts.

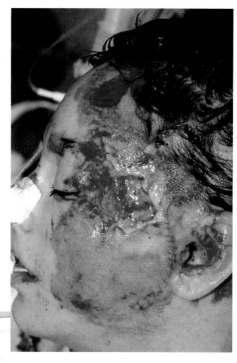

Left, a saline bag was implanted in my cheek in February 2001 to stretch the skin for an upcoming surgery.

Right, banged up and bandaged but still smiling!

04 10 2001

Benefit Concert - July 27, 2000

I made a surprise appearance! Pastor Monty Gravenstein and many friends worked hard to assemble a benefit concert for us at Christ United Methodist Church in Independence, MO. Our dear friends, the Melody Boys Quartet from Arkansas donated their time and talents to make this a wonderful evening. This was the first time I was allowed to leave the Rehabilitation Institute and the first time I had worn nice clothes and makeup in a long time!

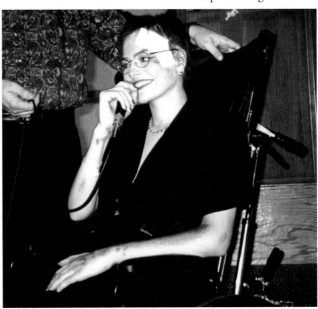

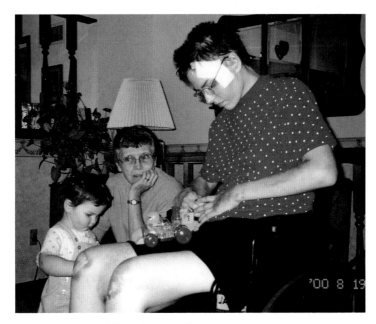

First days at home.

Above, two days after I moved back home, Alisha is fascinated with my wheel-chair. She only ventured this close because Grandma Madalene sat nearby.

Below, Alisha wasn't ready to smile at her birthday party two weeks later.

My home away from home.

Above, Leonard, the receptionist, greeted me with a big smile each day
at the Rehabilitation Institute.

Below, working out on stairs in the therapy gym. Notice the parallel bars
to the left where I took my first step six months earlier!

Celebrating my return to life.

Left, on my 33rd birthday, I was especially thrilled to have both of my sweet little girls on my lap.

04 15 2001

Above and left, Mother's Day 2001. My face is still healing but my daughters don't mind a bit.

Right, the last day of Kindergarten. I stood with only a cane and watched Kayla and friend, Bradford, board the bus.

Recording LIVING PROOF, June 4, 2001.

On the one year anniversary of our accident, Phil and I walked into the recording studio in Nashville. These shots were taken while recording my vocals four days later.

Left, on Alisha's third birthday, I actually managed to get on the floor for an intimate family photo!

Right, what a contrast in photos from Alisha's second birthday to this shot taken a year later at her third birthday party! She is smiling!

Left, on our 11th anniversary, we made it back to our honeymoon spot in Estes Park, Colorado.

Accident re-enactment for the Discovery Health Channel.

Right, Kayla stands "on the set" between a wrecked van and our trailer.

Below, me in my "fake blood" makeup.

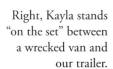

Doug Wix
Chris George
Rae Erickson

It was a joy to be reunited with the actual emergency personel from the accident scene!

Jay Watson

Ministry highlights.

Right, one of our many television appearances, on the set of LIFE TODAY with James and Betty Robison.

Left, our entire crew including Phil's mom and road manager Barb Underwood headed off to sing on a Caribbean cruise.

Right, Major General Carter F. Ham and Major General David H. Hicks of the United States Army give a special presentation at the National Prayer Luncheon.

Photo shoot for our YOU MOVE ME
CD taken April 2008.

Our RELIEF group in December 2006. Still together through it all!

Four generations of the Kleeschulte family, Christmas 2007.

My sisters, Sherry (left) and Cynthia.

The girls and I, along with my mom and dad, Bill and Julia, Christmas 2008.

Christmas with the Morgans.

2002

2004

2008

chapter twelve

Holding On

But Christ is faithful as a son over God's house. And we are his house, if we hold on to our courage and the hope of which we boast.
HEBREWS 3:6

"Hey, look at you!" Phil said, sharing in my excitement.

With a fork secured to my hand, I stabbed a green bean off the lunch tray and brought it to my mouth. Jeanette had brought a gift to my room just in time for lunch – a handy little fabric strap with a pocket to hold a toothbrush, fork, spoon, etc. She slipped the "universal cuff" over my hand and adjusted the Velcro snugly around my palm. Voila! It worked!

I savored the taste, not so much of the green beans – shoot, I would have liked Brussels sprouts at the moment, and I hate Brussels sprouts. No, I relished the flavor of independence. Finally, I could do something for myself!

Jeanette looked up at Phil and smiled.

She set up the rest of my meal, tearing open the sweetener packages, placing the straw in my drink, and arranging my food within easy reach. Everything was fairly easy except for the drink. My weak arms were a bit shaky, so Jeanette stabilized the bottom of the heavy glass as I squeezed it with both palms and brought it to my mouth. I spilled some, but for the most part, I did it myself.

Encouraged by this little taste of independence, hopeful enthusiasm accompanied me into physical therapy. I was determined not to let fear or pessimism take hold. Shannon transferred me to the mat and sat in front of me on her rolling stool.

"OK, we're going to try sitting again," she said. "Try to find your center of balance."

I did my best to assume the tripod position.

"OK," I said.

"You got it?"

"I think so...maybe."

Phil sat next to me, and resisted the urge to help.

"Sit up straight, head up...look at me," Shannon coached.

I pushed my torso up with my arms, straining my shoulders back, and breathing hard. Shannon cautiously released her grip and started the stop watch, her arms inches from mine, on guard to catch me if I faltered.

"You're doing great, Pam! Fifteen seconds...twenty...twenty-five..."

"I'm going down!"

Shannon came to my rescue.

"Thirty-two seconds, Pam! You did it!" she cheered. "Now what we need to work on is this..."

Shannon leaned me back against the wedge and sat up straight with her hands in her lap.

"Yeah, right!" I said. "I don't think so."

So much for avoiding pessimism.

"It will happen," Shannon said. "Give it time."

That was the problem. Time. From the looks of things, my recovery would take a lot of it. On one hand, I had all the time in the world. Madalene was taking good care of the girls for me at home, but I didn't know how long I could stand not being there. My babies were growing up fast, and I was missing it. I couldn't believe how much they had grown in a month. Time was indeed a commodity, and I needed to get better...quickly.

My niece, Debbie, solidified my conviction that afternoon when she brought a collage of pictures to hang on my wall, something she put together as a large "Get Well Soon" sentiment from Kayla and Alisha. The pictures captured moments at her house over the last several weeks, playing dress-up, sitting on the porch swing, eating lunch...even darling shots of Alisha putting little cousin Christopher's pacifier in his mouth and fastening her baby doll into his car seat.

As I gazed at my sweethearts' cute little faces amidst the backdrop of Debbie's home, my heart felt heavy. Her split level house has lots of steps.

"Who knows when I'll be able to go to your house again...if ever," I said, my thoughts becoming audible.

Debbie swung around, tape in hand.

"Hey, none of that!" she chastised.

Her words and tone reminded me of how she used to speak to her mother during Denise's battle with cancer. Powerless to cure her mom's illness, Debbie refused to allow her to give up in despair. Now I was on the receiving end of her admonition.

"I'm looking forward to the day when you're back on stage singing 'God Chooses...'" she said. "Just think about the words: 'God chooses who He uses to do mighty deeds...the broken and ruined are all that He needs.' Sounds prophetic to me."

Yes, I agreed. In fact, Phil and I had discussed this very fact. In jest, I told him he had to quit writing these songs. I didn't know how much more prophecy my body, or my nerves, could take.

We released the song to radio earlier in the year and had just received word it was hitting the top 100 on the charts. How ironic. This was neither a fluke, nor a coincidence. God was doing something. What, I did not know. He hadn't answered that question, and I wasn't sure I could understand it if He did.

Come to think of it, no one had any answers – at least not the ones I was looking for. Especially the able-bodied doctors who really had no idea how it felt to be me.

Monday afternoon, a man who understood my aggravation made his way into my room. Dr. Patrick Caffrey was a neuropsychologist at the Rehabilitation Institute of Kansas City. I noticed his laborious stride. He had the appearance of one who had suffered a stroke, leaving one side weak and droopy and the other compensating. To walk, he hiked his hip and threw out his leg, then dragged the other to catch up. His shoulders drooped a bit, and his neck was stiff. The doctor twisted his entire torso to look over his shoulder. He held a file folder in one hand, and the other arm hung heavily at his side.

If I could just walk like him, I'd be happy, I thought.

Dr. Caffrey introduced himself. He looked at Phil and my parents briefly as he shook their hands, but he quickly shifted his gaze to me. I was clearly the one he wanted to see.

"Hi Pam, I'm Patrick Caffrey," he said, smiling in recognition of my curiosity. "I'm a spinal cord injury survivor myself."

My heart leaped. My mother gasped. Many may have thought him awkward. I thought him beautiful. He could walk.

Dr. Caffrey began to unravel the details of his injury. He broke his neck in a wrestling match as a teenage boy. The location of the injury to his spinal cord was similar to mine, and early on, he could only shrug his shoulders. Describing those days of paralysis with vivid memories, Dr. Caffrey recalled staring at the ceiling counting every stain, every dimple, every crack. He knew them all. Lying flat on his back unable to move, there was simply nothing else to do.

As Dr. Caffrey told story after story that mirrored my own and recounted the timeline of his progress, I grew increasingly excited. Here was someone who knew what I was going through. Someone who could tell me what to expect.

"It's frustrating that no one will give you any straight answers about your future," he said as if reading my mind, "Do you find that to be true?"

"Yes!" I said, amazed at his insight.

Unfortunately, not even Dr. Caffrey could tell me exactly what to expect. He emphasized again that each spinal cord injury is different. Dr. Caffrey's job was not to offer guarantees, but to instill hope of the possible through his personal experience and wisdom. He knew this scary new world. He understood first-hand how it felt for life to fall apart. He faced it years ago. Now this wise counselor stood ready to help me do the same.

From my perspective, two distinct groups co-existed in this rehab environment, the able-bodied and the injured. Either you were disabled, or you weren't. And if you weren't, you were there to help those who were. Period. Until now.

Dr. Caffrey stood out. His presence was a relief and an inspiration. He was the only one who straddled the fence. So many of us from small children to the elderly – victims of strokes, diving accidents, you name it – had been broken and felt ruined. Dr. Caffrey was a beacon of light offering the hope we craved. But I didn't dare admit I needed him.

I didn't need a psychologist, I thought. *I was a Christian, and one in ministry, at that. I was the one who was supposed to help others, not the other way around. God, Phil, and I could handle this just fine all by ourselves.*

Shannon never came right out and said I needed Dr. Caffrey's help, but she praised his work often, especially on days when discouragement had me close to tears. I think she knew I was too proud to initiate a consultation.

All the physical therapists and PT assistants did their best to help. They made me feel like a peer, like a normal human being with a life rather than a disabled patient to treat. Many were also in their early thirties, and we readily joked about life in the 80's and raising our pre-school kids.

Randy worked alongside Shannon, sharing the large blue mat – Shannon and I on one side, and Randy and his patient on the other. I learned about Shannon's one-year-old daughter, Mallory, and Randy's two little boys, one of which was soon to start Kindergarten just like my Kayla. We talked about Phil and our music ministry, and upon finding out that Phil used to sing country music, Randy serenaded me with a snippet of Dolly Parton's, "Jolene."

"Please stop!" I teased.

Randy was known for his unique method of persistence, not only with entertaining patients, but with motivating them to press on through his tough coach approach. Saturday, Randy carried weekend duty, and I wasn't prepared to be part of his team. I was used to Shannon's softer, equally effective technique.

Sitting and holding myself upright on the edge of the mat, Randy announced it was time to advance to a new level. He demonstrated how he wanted me to lower my body sideways and rest my elbow and forearm on the mat. I studied my destination. It was a long way down. Randy assumed the typical therapist position, perched on a stool facing me. I hesitated.

"It's OK, you can do it."

"I don't know..."

"Just go down...like this..." Randy demonstrated again, tipping his trunk quickly and smoothly to his right, mimicking the move.

Easy for you, I thought.

Had this been Shannon, I would have said it out loud, but Randy intimidated me. I didn't want to disappoint him, and I feared failure, not to mention pain. Our face-to-face situation intensified my insecurity. I could see myself falling flat on my wounded face.

"C'mon. You won't fall," Randy continued to insist.

I wasn't so sure. I knew he wasn't supposed to let me fall, but I had never worked with Randy before. He sat back with his hands in his lap. Shannon's outstretched arms always made me feel secure.

Knowing I couldn't escape, I closed my eyes and surrendered, fully expecting my face to hit the mat. Tears stung behind closed eyelids.

I went down...not on the mat, but forward into Randy's lap. How embarrassing. Such a simple request, and I couldn't do it. I bawled. Now I felt weak and stupid – a pathetic, blubbering idiot.

"I'm sorry," I whispered, gasping for air between silent sobs.

"It's OK..."

But it wasn't. Not only did I feel ugly, weak, and helpless, I looked the part as well. I tried to wrestle my emotions back under control, but I couldn't hold myself together. This would have been the perfect time for Dr. Caffrey's help. And yet, I didn't need it, or so I thought.

Fortunately, Dr. Caffrey scheduled a session with me. If Randy had confidentially referred me, the doctor didn't give me that impression. In fact, from the psychologist's perceptions, I ascertained that either he hadn't heard about Saturday's incident, or I had hidden my feelings from Randy better than I thought.

The doc complimented my positive attitude, cooperation, and determination he had observed from a distance the past week. Dr. Caffrey gave me the distinct impression that not all patients were easy to work with. From his descriptions, meltdowns like mine weren't so bad or unusual after all.

"Do you mind telling me how you manage to be so upbeat under the circumstances?" he said.

"God gets me through," I said. "I'm just trying to take it one day at a time."

"Yes," he said, "that's a healthy way to deal with it, and faith certainly helps."

Dr. Caffrey's humble and gentle approach soothed any apprehension I may have harbored prior to our appointment. He sincerely wanted to help, not preach. He even seemed to be looking for something that may help encourage someone else.

"Do you find yourself struggling with certain things more than others?"

Much to my surprise, I unloaded Saturday's nightmarish experience and my fear of further humiliation in PT. I was 32 and couldn't sit up or roll over by myself! My niece's eight-month-old daughter could do more than I!

Dr. Caffrey listened with patient, knowing nods. He'd been there. When I paused to come up for air, Dr. Caffrey presented his neatly tied shoes and impeccably manicured fingernails, emphasizing he had completed both tasks independently with one hand.

"Really," I said. I wasn't sure what that had to do with anything, but I succumbed to follow his lead. "I have to see that."

Dr. Caffrey leaned forward. He pulled the laces and re-tied his shoe with just his right hand. Looking up, he grinned at my open-mouthed astonishment.

"I'm available for parties," he teased.

I chuckled and rolled my eyes apologetically, understanding

what it felt like to be a performing circus animal.

Sitting back in his chair, Dr. Caffrey raised his eyebrows and lifted his index finger. There was more.

"Not long ago during a discussion with my friend, Ce Abbey, I shared there was one thing I couldn't do – open a jar of spaghetti sauce," he said. "Immediately Ce scolded me. 'Shame on you!' she said to me. 'That's just one thing you haven't figured out how to do *yet*.'"

Dr. Caffrey continued his story, confessing that her challenge pushed him to accomplish the task. Miming the act as he described the steps, he lowered a pretend jar onto the floor and lodged it between the chair leg and his strong foot. With his able hand, Dr. Caffrey twisted the lid, and... Voila!

I was impressed, to say the least, but I wondered what these stories and feats had to do with me now. Seeing "I don't get it" in my eyes, Dr. Caffrey tried an analogy.

"Weight builds muscle, right?"

I nodded.

"Okay, weights are heavy, and the exertion is difficult, but we lift them, push against them, and resist them because we know that's what builds strength," he said. "And the stronger we become, the easier and lighter the weight feels. So we add more weight to build more strength."

I had no idea at the time how biblical was Dr. Caffrey's counsel. Romans 5:3-4 says, "*...we also rejoice in our sufferings, because we know that suffering produces perseverance; perseverance, character; and character, hope.*" Dr. Caffrey's stories and demonstrations perfectly exemplified how his perseverance developed his character and gave him hope.

"Extreme difficulty is an opportunity for growth. If everything was easy for you, there'd be no hope. You'd have nowhere else to go. But as it is, your difficulty is an opportunity for you to improve, to soar to new heights...and from the looks of things you are," he said, referring to how I wheeled into his office just a few moments before.

Dr. Caffrey's words spoke layers of wisdom. Yet at the time, I thought he spoke merely of my physical progress. Compared to his amazing accomplishments, I didn't think wheeling myself around was very impressive. But the counselor's point hit home.

Dr. Caffrey's abilities didn't happen overnight. He worked long, grueling months, even years, to rebuild his life, piece by piece. Just as it had built Dr. Caffrey's strength, physical therapy would build my strength in many ways. And just like him, I would adjust, learning new ways to adapt to life with a disability.

When I first saw Dr. Caffrey, I noticed his stride and gross motor abilities. I saw the limp. I saw the stiffness. I saw the brace on his leg. After I got to know him, I saw someone I wanted to be. In my eyes he was no longer a man with only half of his body working. He was a man of strength – living, working, helping others, and loving it. His life was not defined by his disability or restricted by inability. Even with all of his limitations, he was free!

Clumsily I wheeled into the gym. My shoulders ached from the strain of wheeling my body weight across the floor. But my spirit housed new motivation. Today's pain and tedious persistence would bring tomorrow's freedom.

Still rehearsing Dr. Caffrey's captivating demonstration in my mind, I wondered if someday my example would be just as powerful. If so, I had a long way to go. Dr. Caffrey's perspective gave me good reason to persevere. When dread and discouragement threatened to loosen my grip, I could only pray that God would give me the strength to hold on.

The Easy Way Out

You need to persevere so that when
you have done the will of God, you will
receive what he has promised.

HEBREWS 10:36

"Rise and shine!"

Nurses on their six o'clock morning rounds burst through my door. After weeks of hearing someone spout that phrase every morning, I came to hate the very words. They made me want to curse, and I hate foul language. I couldn't rise, at least not by myself, and what in the world was there worth shining for? The first rays of daylight streamed through the cracks in the blinds. Dread dropped like a bomb. Ugh! Another day.

I much preferred nighttime. Especially on non-shower nights. In those dark hours, nothing was expected of me until morning, and I could disappear into the silly antics of the "Frasier" characters on TV. A double hitter of the dysfunctional psychotherapist and his family provided a pleasant distraction from reality before hiding all night long in the healthy body of my dreams.

I shut my eyes again, trying to push back the dawn and escape once again. But even through my closed eyelids, the sunlit world refused to let me return to the ease I found in slumber. Sounds of scrubbing teeth and water rushing into the sink in preparation for

Mom's and Phil's shift change drifted from the bathroom. Noisy medicine carts squeaked and rambled down the hall for morning wake-up rounds. Overhead intercom speakers called, "Room 215 needs assistance." Oh, the annoying reminders of disabled life at the institute.

It would have been easy to snap at anyone and everyone who greeted me with such cheer every morning. But instead, I did my best to swallow my disgust and put a smile on my face and in my voice.

"Good morning...," I said, which was another lie. What was so good about it?

Perhaps these very words churning in my stomach were partly to blame for my intense bouts of nausea every morning. The doctors implicated reflux, but I wasn't convinced. Medication sitting on an empty stomach for two hours is enough to make anyone sick. Breakfast didn't arrive until eight.

By nine, Cathie, my regular Occupational Therapist, stood at my bedside for Adult Daily Living Skills (ADLS), teaching me how to get my heavy, lifeless body ready in the morning. It was during this first therapy session of the day that the rubber really hit the road, so to speak. I quickly learned how degrading it is to lose the use of your hands. Case in point – getting dressed. No longer a private affair, Cathie stood close, ready to assist if I needed her. She raised the head of my bed as far as it would go. A bra was out of the question – too difficult. But from a sitting position, I learned to pull a shirt over my head fairly quickly as my right arm had decent strength and flexibility. Cathie introduced me to a small device that strapped over my palm and made buttons pretty easy. Pants, socks, and shoes, on the other hand, were an entirely different story.

Cathie coached as I attempted to lasso my foot with a long canvas strap sporting a loop on each end. With the smaller loop around my wrist, I captured my foot with the other and dragged it close to my body. Frustration grew as I tried to stuff my toe and heel through the elastic ankle of my sweat pants. With each attempt, my heavy foot seemed to sink further into the bed. Suddenly, in a moment of genius, I shoved my arm under my ankle, lifted my foot over my other leg, and rested my ankle on top of my thigh.

"Way to go, Pam," Cathie cheered, "Good creativity, keep it up."

Eventually I maneuvered the sweats around both ankles, and began to pull them up. But getting them over my hips was an insurmountable feat; I couldn't grip the waistband or roll myself from side to side to inch them up. Cathie usually helped with this part to keep my frustration and endurance in check. But then came the socks. Nearly thirty minutes had passed once I finally finagled one stupid sock over my toe. I couldn't take it any longer!

"Why can't Phil just do this for me?"

"What happens if he's not there when you want to get dressed?" she said. "Do you want to depend on him or someone else to dress you forever?"

Cathie didn't really want an answer, but I gave her one anyway.

"No, but let's work on it when I'm stronger," I said, annoyed. "This is such a waste of time."

Cathie knew better, yet seeing I had reached my limit, she helped me with my shoes, hoisted me into the chair, and watched me wheel into the bathroom to brush my teeth. By this time, Cathie and I had gotten to know each other well. With a world of wisdom she took my protests in stride, insisting day after day that I try again, always knowing when to help and when to push me to do it myself.

At ten o'clock I was ready to start a full day's schedule – an hour each of physical and occupational therapy, an hour lunch, another hour of PT and OT, and an hour of group exercise. Group counseling and a "Meet your New Body" health class also met for an hour each at least once during the week.

"Excel" was an optional supervised exercise program which met at the end of the day, and was open to the entire disabled community, not just the patients. With equipment specifically designed for the handicapped, lifting and pushing weights reaped benefits beyond the physical. Exercising with others further along in the recovery process – and more accustomed to their injuries

– made me feel like I belonged. I was fascinated by their stories and loved picking their brains about how they handled life. It felt good to be with people who understood my struggle.

Matt Wise was one such individual with a name behooving his character. This slender, bearded red-head was a seven-year veteran quad in a bulky, well-worn power chair. The sound of his motor was so loud and distinct, the entire gym knew Matt had arrived while he was still thirty feet down the hall.

Usually clad in a white sleeveless t-shirt, ball cap, jeans, and hiking boots, Matt was friendly and compassionate...and mischievous. Placing his wheelchair on high speed, Matt spun himself in circles until he almost flung himself from his chair. Sometimes he'd race another friend down the hallway when no one was looking. He'd scare me half to death one minute and then turn around to ask me how I was doing the next.

Matt was indeed an interesting character, and talented. Everyone in the gym recognized Matt's creativity for making the hardest tasks easier. His engineering mind designed gadgets (adaptive devices) to help with all kinds of physical disabilities, and his skilled, able-bodied roommate built them. Therapists constantly sought his wisdom and how-to advice. There didn't seem to be anything he couldn't do.

Matt loved a challenge, and he enjoyed presenting others with the same. One day as we worked out, he noticed my shoe buttons. Cathie had screwed a little knob into the last lace hole of each shoe, looped the laces around the knobs and tied them tightly so that it would be easy for me to get my shoes on and off without tying the laces myself. All I had to do was hook my thumb into the loop and slip the already tied laces around the knobs.

"What are those?" Matt said.

I was surprised the king of adaptive devices had never seen them. I glanced at his shoes. They were neatly tied without shoe buttons.

"Cathie gave these to me so all I have to do is hook the ties over the buttons," I said.

"Why?" he said.

"You ought to know," I said. "So I can do it myself!"

"Let me see your hands," he said, dismissing my comment.

Apprehensively I held them out.

"How much can you move your fingers?"

I had started to move them slightly, enough to draw my thumb in laterally toward my palm to touch the side of my index finger, but since I couldn't apply any pressure, it was a far cry from a useful grip.

"You have more strength than I do," he retorted, "and I tied my shoes all by myself."

Matt untied his shoes and showed me step by step how he did it. Suddenly I knew how Dr. Caffrey felt when Ce challenged him to the spaghetti jar task. As I watched, I wasn't sure I liked Matt's lesson; Cathie's way was much easier.

Adaptive devices were great. Matt had tons of them, but he had learned to use them only when absolutely necessary. Living with a disability requires keen discernment to know when to push and when to hold back because the risk is too great. If safety is a concern (as when using a knife or scissors), by all means, use common sense and avoid injury. And if frustration becomes overwhelming, take a break. Use the device before all motivation is permanently destroyed. The key is to gradually move forward, not lose ground.

Like Dr. Caffrey, Matt had learned that great things are rarely achieved by always taking the easy way out. Doing so limits our opportunity and our growth. It can even make us cowards, afraid to try something new – content with less than God wants for us. I pleaded for a miracle, but if God said, "Pam, pick up your mat and walk," would I have the guts to do it? Or would I say, "No thanks, that's too hard." Indeed it was too hard for me, but was it too hard for God? I could just picture Matt asking, "How big is this God of yours anyway?"

Matt's lesson scared the daylights out of me, but I refused to let fear paralyze me more than it had already. I *could* do more for myself. I could learn to put on my *own* socks and tie my *own* shoes.

The intense physical effort required by working alongside my insightful friend – together with my body's healing – turned me into a calorie burning machine. I ate well and still lost weight. Of course, dwindling muscle mass significantly contributed to my shrinking figure, but raging metabolism also shared responsibility. If there was a benefit to working my body until it was dog tired every day, that was it. I could eat whatever I wanted, as much as I wanted. Too bad that didn't last.

On the other hand, some things did seem to last forever. Nurses on their six o'clock morning rounds bursting through my door. Dread dropping like a bomb, as heavily as the day before. Day after day of enduring the never-ending routine.

It certainly would have been easy to snap at anyone and everyone who walked through my door in those first hours of daylight. It would have been easy to dismiss Cathie and let my family dress me every morning. My biggest battle was to avoid the temptation to take the easy way out. At the time, all my hard work didn't appear to move me any closer to winning the war against paralysis, or sending me to the place where I was sure life would be easier... home.

chapter fourteen

Perfect Timing

He is your praise; he is your God, who has
done for you these great and awesome things
that your own eyes have seen.
DEUTERONOMY 10:21

No medication could dull the agony when Kayla and Alisha walked out the door. I loved seeing my little girls' sweet faces once a week when they visited, but our time together always disappeared too quickly, and watching them leave killed me.

Usually I managed to stuff the heart-wrenching emotions for Mom's sake during her shifts. Yet truthfully, I stifled them for mine as well. Mom knows my vulnerable side better than anyone, and I was afraid if I allowed my weakness and tears to break through with her, I would get lost in sorrow and never find my way out. I actually got pretty good at feigning positive attitudes and spouting platitudes. But one evening insult added to injury – literally – and pushed me over the edge, leaving my heart shattered into smithereens.

Mom arrived, and Phil prepared to leave when my mother-in-law showed up with the girls. They often met Daddy at the end of his shifts to visit for awhile. This time out-of-town relatives accompanied them. I knew they were coming, but I wasn't prepared for the ensuing clamor. The small room quickly overflowed with people and chaotic conversation. I enjoyed reconnecting with Phil's cousins, but I longed most of all to spend a few quality moments with my girls, now distracted by all the commotion. Each passing second I knew the time of our dreaded separation drew closer.

"How about dinner at Timberline Steakhouse?" Phil suggested over the hubbub.

The group enthusiastically agreed, and I felt a fiery stab in my chest. My favorite restaurant! I looked at my husband in shock, but he didn't notice. How could the love of my life be so insensitive? I was invisible to this chatty, hungry bunch, my room merely a gathering place for their family reunion.

I waited for Phil's extended family to considerately allow me a few minutes alone with him and the girls to say our goodbyes. Nothing doing. The river of visitors that meandered through my doorway reversed its course, and drifted out with a casual farewell, sweeping the girls away in their current. Phil lingered a moment longer, but dinner beckoned, and his empty stomach was like a hook pulling him out the door. Not knowing where to begin, and not wanting to ruin his evening, I said nothing.

He kissed me and left. I was crushed. I felt betrayed. I wanted to cry out to God, but the heaviness was so sickening, I couldn't think. I couldn't find words that even began to describe the pain, the loneliness, the despair. All I could do was hurt...and sob.

I could tell Mom wanted to cradle her youngest baby in her arms as she watched me weep without holding back. I didn't care if I cried all night. I let it all go, diving head first into the pit of sorrow. Mom instinctively threw out her safety net of compassion. She held my hand and stroked my hair, knowing I wasn't just upset about dinner. This one night, added to all the others, seemed to carry a life sentence. A permanent decree that I would forever be confined – held back, left out of my own life. It was an unfair verdict, and one that I could do nothing about.

"My entire world just walked out that door," I wailed.

In the midst of my breakdown, the phone rang. My sister, Cynthia, announced to Mom that she and her family were on their way and would be there in about thirty minutes. Her husband,

Don, had some questions for me...about my faith. When Mom hung up the phone, she reluctantly told me they were coming. I couldn't believe it.

"Great," I said sarcastically, "perfect timing."

Through the years my sister seemed to have a knack for showing up at the wrong time. I wanted to see her – just not like this, not tonight. I prayed for composure and did my best to put on a happy face.

When they walked through the door, Mom took my little nephew, Matt, outside to walk through the hospital's flower garden across the street. Cynthia and Don pulled chairs close to my bed, wanting to know all the latest news from rehab. As soon as the chitchat died down, Don started to explain what he really came to ask. He had sensed peace in our family after my oldest sister's death from cancer three years before, and right on the heels of her passing, he saw it again after her son's tragic demise in a car accident. Now Don said he witnessed the same cool assurance...in me.

"I don't understand it," he said. "How can you be so calm when your world just fell apart?"

"Ha!" I blurted.

The irony was dumbfounding. During one of my lowest moments since the accident, Don asked about *peace*. I had to fess up. I couldn't fill him with a line of baloney and ignore the truth, especially considering how I was anything but calm, cool, and collected a few moments ago. Besides, I didn't have the strength or desire to build a facade.

"Things aren't always what they seem," I said. "Truth be known, I ache inside. I hate what happened to me."

Don was confused. I paused for a few seconds to think...

I will remember the deeds of the LORD... PSALMS 77:11

*...tell of all his wonderful acts. Remember the
wonders he has done...* PSALMS 105:2, 5

115

"Who God is to me has not changed because my body doesn't work or because I don't like the situation," I said, carefully choosing my words. "I can't turn away from God because my life hasn't worked out as I planned. God has always been there for me, and He's the only one who can help me now, so why would I shun Him?

Don listened intently as I recapped how my relationship with God began. Raised in the Lutheran church, the pastor read Matthew 6:33 as I kneeled at the altar to accept Christ during confirmation, "But seek first [God's] kingdom and his righteousness, and all these things will be given to you as well."

"God impressed upon me this verse was truth I needed to heed closely," I said. "When I first heard it, I thought maybe God would make me rich if I followed Him."

I laughed. "OK, so maybe material wealth wasn't exactly what He had in mind. But as an adult, I've grown to understand that God knows my needs and will provide. As long as I keep Him first in my life, I don't need to worry. He'll take care of me."

Don looked bewildered.

"That may sound unrealistic," I said, "but God has proven it. No one can argue God's provision when they look at me. Honestly, how many people survive hitting the highway at 70 miles an hour? And not only that, what are the chances that a nurse, respiratory therapist, and anesthesiologist would just happen to be passing by the scene and stop to help? There is no such thing as coincidence, I'm convinced."

Cynthia knowingly nodded as I continued to illustrate God's hand in my life. Three months before the accident, my employer downsized, and my family was suddenly without health insurance. We took out personal health insurance policies for each of us, but never heard a word from the company. Two days after the wreck, our insurance cards arrived in the mail, showing coverage commenced two weeks before. We since discovered the new company had *no limitation* on physical therapy! As an employee in the insurance industry, Don marveled.

"*That's* a miracle," he said.

"Yes, it is," I said. "God is working around us all the time. For example…"

I described that a couple of years before, Phil and I were looking for a used, full-sized, 8-cylinder conversion van to replace our minivan. Without telling anyone the amount we needed, we received a donation to cover it, to the penny. We got just what we were looking for – low mileage, beautiful comfort, a powerful engine – and we didn't spend a cent.

"Unfortunately, that blessing is now in the junkyard, but you won't believe the check we just got! God took care of us again."

A couple saw the story of our accident in an area newspaper. They, too, had been involved in an accident and recently received a settlement that exceeded what was necessary to replace their vehicle. So they sent the overage to us. The amount matched almost exactly what we lacked to replace our van with a brand new model, wheelchair lift-equipped.

My audience was engrossed, as was I. Each story spurred another, building a case for God's indisputable presence and timely provision.

"Indeed, I've learned Matthew 6:33 first-hand," I said, "and my definition of 'these things will be added to you' has broadened dramatically. True wealth lies in the love of family and friends – and of course, that of my Heavenly Father. You know, brushes with tragedy always make what really matters in life perfectly clear. I may not like every turn of events, but I know God loves me. He's in charge, and that's all I need to know."

Suddenly I realized a drastic change. Cynthia and Don intended their visit for their benefit, and I pray it was. But it was also for mine. I needed to remember that God was my provider, comforter, encourager, and confidante…my very best friend. I needed to see that the hard realities of the past three months paled in comparison to the fact that God's power supersedes all. Period. And neither He, nor His love, ever changes…no matter what. Rehearsing my history with God completely eradicated the stronghold of despair that clutched me only an hour before. And in its place I found a surprising surge of strength, certainty, joy, and yes, even peace. My dear sister's infamous ability to call at the worst possible time was, as it turned out, perfect timing indeed. God's perfect timing.

I Didn't Fit

Do not conform any longer to the pattern of this
world, but be transformed by the renewing of your
mind. Then you will be able to test and approve what
God's will is – his good, pleasing and perfect will.

ROMANS 12:2

"What happened to her, Mommy?"

A curious child pointed at me from his stroller as the elevator door opened. His embarrassed mother immediately hushed him.

"Shhh!" she said and whisked him away as soon as the way was clear. The little boy's honesty cooled my excitement like the fountains across the street tempered the sidewalk's heat.

I had been released to take my first "day trip" outside the Institute, and I was ecstatic as we arrived at Crown Center, one of Kansas City's high class, downtown malls. Barefoot children dodged in and out of the fountains, screaming playfully as geysers randomly spurted into the air and fell back to slap the pavement. Phil pushed me past them toward a clear glass wall that stood between us and an expansive foyer.

Once inside, we paused briefly to take in the sight; multiple levels of lofty storefronts brimmed with busy weekend shoppers. I couldn't believe I was here.

Phil quickened his pace down the shiny tile ramp in search of an elevator, avoiding the wall of escalators. He gave me a thrilling ride, zooming through the crowd, careful not to take anyone out along the way. We laughed at the alarmed faces, unsure whether they feared getting hurt, or if they feared Phil would hurt me.

Now at the elevator, the child's blunt question evoked an unexpected awkwardness. Instantly I realized I stuck out like a sore thumb. Baggy sweats, no make-up, and a hospital bracelet were enough to warrant a sideways glance, but adding a neck brace, facial bandages, and thick, red scars on my forearm to the picture induced shocked stares.

"Don't worry about them," Phil said, backing me inside the elevator. "This is our day. Don't let them get you down."

At that moment, I made a decision to be normal. Quadriplegic? Yes. Different? Yes. And normal. Phil was right. This was a date, and I wanted to enjoy it as much as he did. There were no doctors, no nurses, no well-wishing visitors. No therapy, no classes. Just Phil and me, and a whole day of nothing to do but enjoy each other. So when people stared, I smiled. When a retail saleswoman asked Phil what size I wore, I answered kindly. When a child pointed, I waved. Choosing to rise above the circumstances made a distinct difference. Each act of grace returned another – a held door, unsolicited help in carrying food or drink. Time after time we found kindness. And I couldn't remember when we had as much fun.

Phil and I took in all of the attractions, seeing everything, including each other, with newfound appreciation. We felt like teenagers again, experiencing every sparkling detail as if for the very first time. Wandering along the storefronts and restaurants, Phil and I reminisced of how we met here years ago. Crown Center became our special place, and now it seemed even more so. We ate dinner at the same quaint little streetcar restaurant we loved so much, and the food tasted even better than we remembered. Back then we strolled hand-in-hand through the halls, now Phil pushed my wheelchair along – something we had only pictured decades in the future, when we grew old and feeble. But I didn't care. We were together. And that was enough.

After dinner, Phil wheeled me into the movie theater upstairs and found a perfect private spot for us in the back – an end seat with enough space alongside for my wheelchair. We both wanted to see this newly released comedy, and as the lights dimmed, we were almost giddy to actually see it together on the big screen. But a fresh dose of pain medication prior to opening credits soon made me groggy. Sitting warm, snug, and secure next to the man I loved, I fell asleep straight up in my chair.

As the story progressed, I failed to laugh during the funny scenes, Phil glanced over to see if I was alright. My head was still poised upright as if I were watching the movie (thanks to the neck brace), but my eyes were shut.

"Pam," Phil whispered. I didn't answer.

"Pam," he whispered again. Still, no answer.

Growing frantic, Phil finally shouted, "Pam!"

I awoke, startled. "What, what, what?"

Phil sank back into his chair, relieved. I chuckled at the look on his face. I scared him half to death!

"Are you OK?" I said, bringing the conversation back to a whisper. People started to stare at the disturbance.

"Yes, are you?" he said, amused, but still breathing heavily. "For a moment there, well…I thought you were a goner!"

Phil and I giggled the rest of the evening every time we thought about it. This wonderful day would be engrained on our memories forever. I couldn't remember enjoying anything as much, possibly ever. I didn't want it to end.

Unfortunately, the hours passed all too quickly, and we had to go. As the driver loaded me into the rear of the transport van once again, he strapped me in, and chained me down. The old devastating truth resurfaced. Phil climbed into the front passenger seat, out of ear-shot and out of reach. So much for intimate travel conversation. I couldn't hear squat back there. I hated it. How humiliating. Alone I watched the lively scenes of Crown Center grow smaller and smaller as the driver pulled away. Alone, I feared I would forever be hauled around like cargo. The date was over.

Four weeks had come and gone since I transferred from the hospital to rehab, and still, the goals for sending me home seemed distant. We may have survived a few hours at Crown Center, but surviving permanently at home was a completely different story.

"How much longer will it take?" I asked.

"A few more weeks," came the unchanging, vague reply.

"FOREVER," is what I heard.

I couldn't begin to roll over in bed or transfer myself. I was the thinnest I had ever been, yet my body felt like it weighed a thousand pounds. I needed a lot of help, much more than Shannon's goal of "moderate assistance."

Even if I had been physically ready to go home, our house wasn't. After a quick visit to our modest three-bedroom raised-ranch, Shannon and Cathie made a list of obstacles that seemed endless: a full set of stairs at each entrance, narrow hallways, even narrower doorways, basement laundry facilities, round, slick doorknobs impossible for me to grasp, and on and on...

"A stairglide alone will run somewhere in the neighborhood of $3,000," Shannon said.

Health insurance wouldn't cover any of the necessary home modifications, but it wasn't the money that concerned me. God would provide. What I dreaded was the time it would take to get it all done. Projects like this don't happen overnight.

"How long will that take?"

"Don't worry about it. It *will* get done," Phil promised. You *will* come home."

"How? I can't even get into the car."

We were down to one vehicle, our little red, 4-door Toyota Camry. It barely held us and our two young daughters. A wheelchair would never fit, and transferring me into the front seat would be extremely difficult, if not impossible.

I thought back to our day at Crown Center, to the happy, carefree kids dancing through the fountains. And I winced again at the thought of the child's shocked expression in the elevator. I felt his pointing finger that drew all attention to me, the freak in the wheelchair. Everywhere strangers and stares, obstacles and missed opportunities all screamed the obvious – I didn't fit in the world anymore.

Get Me Out of Here!

Oh, GOD, my Lord, step in; work a
miracle for me… Get me out of here…

PSALMS 109:21 (MSG)

"My baby girl's second birthday is in two weeks, and I want to be home by then," I announced boldly.

"Hmmm…" Dr. Berger said, studying my chart. Then with a sly grin, "I think that can be arranged."

"Really?" I shrieked in surprise. *Wow! That was easy*, I thought. *I should have asked sooner.*

Dr. Berger seemed amused by my sudden outburst of enthusiasm. But it was no wonder, I had no idea he would agree. He had given no indication that he thought I was ready. I didn't really know if I *was* ready; I just wanted to go home. I was tired of missing out on my daughters' lives. And that's all that mattered. Well, almost.

Dr. Berger's decision set everyone in motion. All my therapists prepared my family and me to make the transition as smooth as possible, all the while warning me that going home might not be as joyful as I thought.

"This is going to be the hardest thing you've done yet," Shannon and Cathie said.

Transferring, showering, dressing, toileting, and changing

123

bandages were just the beginning of a long list that would be completely up to us. No back-up nurse would be available if we were tired or in a bind. Home would look and feel completely different from a wheelchair.

Yeah, yeah, yeah, I thought, hearing their words, but not knowing what they meant and not really caring. My tunnel vision focused only on the comforts of home. Everything was always better at home. I became more certain of this as one by one, Phil and I achieved every goal on the list that became my passport out of there. With each accomplishment, I was sure that joy was right around the corner.

But one final matter of business to take care of cracked my confidence and rattled me so much, it threatened to ruin everything. The uneasiness I felt was like stepping onto a rickety old bridge, then suddenly realizing it was my only protection against falling into a bottomless dark abyss.

"Pam, this is Jerry," Shannon said as she approached with a tall, nicely dressed, bald man. "He's here to measure you for your new wheelchair."

Suddenly I felt nauseated with dread. I didn't want to need the stinkin' chair in the first place. I tried to force a smile.

Jerry opened his attaché case and pulled out a tape measure. He stretched it against my legs – hips to knees, knees to heels, noting the figures carefully. He grabbed his clipboard, scribbled some notes, and began the barrage of questions. How did I intend to use the chair? Indoors only? Inside and out? Would I need a tray? How about footrests – individuals that swing out and detach, or a single plate that flips up and down? What other accessories would I need?

Oh no, I thought. *I can't do this. Not alone.*

I hesitated, hating that Phil wasn't there. I trusted his judgment on such decisions; he was better at seeing the big picture. Besides, I was taking one day at a time, focusing on progress. But this… this forced me to think about days, months, perhaps even… I shuddered. No, no, no, no, no. I couldn't go there. The thought hurt too much. I had already forced myself to accept that my original goal of leaving rehab without the wheelchair wasn't going to happen. But an easier life at home was still my dream. It was my hope. And I couldn't let go of hope. It's all that made the present bearable.

"Pam?" Shannon's voice snapped me back to reality.

My eyes filled with tears. Recognizing I was close to a break down, Shannon did her best to help me muddle through the evaluation, answering for me whenever she could.

"Okay," Jerry said, "One final question."

"Thank God!" I said, and suddenly realized, horrified, that I said it aloud. "Oh my gosh, I'm sorry!"

"It's alright," Jerry smiled with understanding. "I've heard worse. Trust me, I know this hasn't been easy. Now…what color would you like?"

"That's easy." I said, relieved to feel certain about something. "Purple. It's my husband's favorite color."

Hope Deferred

Hope deferred makes the heart sick…

PROVERBS 13:12

"There she is, Miss America!" Leonard beamed from his post at the front desk, "Are you coming back to see me?"

"Outpatient therapy starts Monday," I said.

"I'll be waiting, you gorgeous thing you!"

I could always count on our beloved receptionist to make me smile, but today I hardly heard Leonard's gushing sentiment. All I could think about was reuniting my family. Everything was packed -- all the cards, flowers, pictures, and wall hangings. Large plastic shopping bags and trash sacks overflowed with medical supplies and adaptive devices, all ready to go – and so was I.

The drive home felt odd. I noticed every detail along the familiar highways – new road construction projects, newly planted trees, new billboards advertising new restaurants and new TV shows… The sights were surreal. Winding around the curves of our neighborhood, I pondered how three months of my life had vanished. The lush vegetation that I remembered of early summer was now dry and turning brown, and the trees looked as tired as I felt. It was as if I fell asleep in early June and woke up in late

August. The world around me pressed on, weathering a long, dry summer, and I missed it.

Finally, home popped into view. I nearly cried. Passing mostly drab and dry yards of our neighbors, I expected to see a yard displaying three months of neglect. Instead, brilliant color welcomed us. Vibrant impatiens spilled from their beds, accenting a freshly cut lawn and neatly trimmed bushes.

"Wow!" Phil said. "Joe has been mowing the grass, and he said he's had some help, but...wow!"

Ah, Joe. All that work, all for this moment. I was honored.

Phil eased the car into our dark basement garage, and the immensity of my disabilities glared. The Institute was designed for the disabled. This place was not. Phil struggled to transfer me out of the car. I wheeled easily across the cement floor, but once inside the basement door, thick Berber carpet held my wheels like glue.

"Hang on!" Phil said, unpacking the car, "Don't wear yourself out before we get upstairs!"

Not listening, I strained harder. Nothing would push those tires forward.

Phil hurried over and plopped bags into my lap. "I *said*, 'Wait!'" He sounded only mildly frustrated as he easily pushed me through the basement.

Show off, I thought.

For a moment the familiarity of home enveloped me in comfort. Then we rounded the corner to the stairwell. The choking cloud of doubt and fear was back. A mountain loomed before me.

"You've got to be kidding," I said as I beheld our newly installed stair lift. "I can't sit in that. I'll fall out!"

Phil sat in the tiny seat, demonstrating. "See? You won't fall out."

"*You* are not paralyzed," I said, like he needed reminding. "Of course, *you* wouldn't fall out."

"And neither will you."

Amidst my cries of resistance, Phil transferred me to the tiny vinyl chair. My long heavy legs draped several inches beyond the short seat, and my back towered above the miniscule backrest, leaving little to lean against.

"My butt is gonna slide right out!"

"You'll be fine," Phil said, "I've got you." He fastened the seatbelt and cinched it snugly around my waist.

"What is that supposed to do? Hold me onto this thing?"

Phil propped my feet on the footrest, ignoring my sarcasm, and said, "Now, hold tight while I carry the wheelchair upstairs."

"Hurry," I whined, not knowing how long I could sit without toppling over.

Within seconds, Phil bounded up the steps, set the wheelchair in place, and hurried back down to quiet my whimpering.

"Now push the 'up' button, right there," he said, nodding toward the armrest.

Finding the control, I palmed the arrow that pointed up. The sudden jerk startled me.

"I'm not going to let you fall," Phil bellowed over my wailing. "Just don't look down!"

Phil stayed right with me all the way up, climbing the stairs slowly and holding me in as I inched up the track. At the top, he released a lever that turned the seat ninety degrees. When my feet rested securely on the upper landing, Phil kneeled and took my trembling body in his arms. I buried my head in his shoulder and cried.

"Why did God spare my life only to leave me like THIS?? How am I going to face this terror every day?"

"You're fine! You did it! You see? You're OK!" Phil soothed, wrapping me in comfort. I drank in my husband's embrace as he stroked my back. "Are you ready to go further?"

No! I thought to myself, but kept silent. Phil was perfect. He didn't push me to answer, he just held me until I gradually caught my breath and gained composure.

"Alright, let's go."

Phil transferred me to the wheelchair, and I caught a glimpse of the dining room table in the adjoining room. What a mess!

"Take me over there."

As we approached the table, the clutter became clear.

Scrapbooking materials lay in disarray, just as I left them three months earlier. My scrapbook was open to Kayla's 5th birthday page. We celebrated just days before the accident, the layout – still incomplete. My pen rested across my handwritten journal, documenting every joy of that day. Cropped photos lay loose. Sadness engulfed me, and a tear rolled down my cheek. Images of Kayla – blowing out her candles, flying kites with Daddy, hugging me… I paused at the last. Kneeling in the grass, I wrapped one arm around my big birthday girl and held a kite in the other. Kayla rested her head on my shoulder with a look that said, "This is the best day ever!" It was the perfect shot of my perfect life – a healthy, happy mommy and her sweet little girl. In fact, all of the pictures were flawless images of my ideal former life – one that was now impossible to repeat. Or record.

Phil insightfully pulled my chair away and headed for the kitchen. As we crossed the threshold into the spaciousness of ivory and blue country charm, I remembered slaving for weeks in the spring. I cleaned out cabinets and drawers, purged what was no longer needed, and organized the rest.

I savored the warmth of the west sun streaming in the window of my favorite room and re-acquainted myself, as if catching up with an old friend. The pretty oak cabinetry, our shiny new dishwasher, the old stove whose clock never worked. Ah, a steaming cup of coffee sounded so good right now. Vanilla nut crème, fully caffeinated, one sweetener.

My coffeemaker sat back on the counter top, distant against the ivory tile backsplash. Beside it, my favorite cup hung on the mug tree I got for Christmas. Both were covered in dust – silent, as if betrayed, wondering where I had been, patiently waiting for our leisurely Bible studies at the breakfast table. I glanced down at my helpless fingers. It looked as though they'd have to wait a little longer.

I couldn't wait to see the girls' bedrooms. I had to wait a little longer to actually see the girls, as we thought it best to have one day of adjustment alone. In the meantime, I wanted to surround myself with their scents, their stuff, their space. I wanted to refamiliarize myself with every nook and cranny. I wanted to remember our tender moments tucking them in at night – backs scratched, prayers prayed, and cheeks kissed.

We crept down the hall, and the walls, lined with family photographs, seemed to close in. Bulky wheels, footrests and Phil's towering frame swallowed up the shrinking space. As we approached Alisha's room, the door seemed much narrower than I remembered. My wheelchair would never make the turn. No way.

"How are we going to…," I began. With a stroke of ingenuity, Phil lifted the back end of my chair and turned it ninety degrees. "Just like that, I guess."

As gently as possible, Phil inched me through the door. I cringed as my wheels scraped the wooden frame. *Phil may have to brush up on his home repair skills,* I thought.

We stopped just inside the door, unable to go any further. Toys peppered the floor, just as Alisha left them. Many were turned upside down, including the Little Tikes piano with multi-colored plastic keys at my feet. Most likely she had turned it over and touched each screw pensively, as if trying to figure out how to take it apart.

With his foot, Phil shoved aside the toys of our budding engineer and slowly turned me full-circle. I absorbed my sweet Alisha's world. Cuddly teddy bears sat on guard atop her shelves, and embroidered ones peered from wall hangings. Her white crib sat in the corner, the aqua sheet still wrinkled from her restless slumber. Above it, yellow wooden letters playfully spelled her name on the pale blue wall.

Originally Kayla's nursery, I smiled to think of how we painted the walls blue when I was pregnant with her. I was confident I was having a boy, but as soon as we finished, I knew my maternal intuition had deceived me. Instead of re-painting, I accessorized with anything and everything girly – pastel colors, frilly gingham curtains and quilts, floppy-eared bunnies, and cross-stitched birth announcements. Now teddy bears and blue better suited my tomboyish toddler.

My favorite photograph of Phil and ten-month-old Alisha rested on the child-sized chest of drawers that used to be her Daddy's. They hugged cheek-to-cheek, with their tongues hanging out at the camera. I loved taking that picture and capturing the silliness as Alisha imitated everything Daddy did.

Squeezing back through the doorway, we left a matching set of wheelchair scratches, deeper than the first. We didn't even bother entering Kayla's room at the end of the hall. No doubt, I'd get stuck. It required two tight turns to enter, one right after the other. At the very least, it would surely cause more damage than we cared to fix.

I sighed and peeked inside her powder pink room. The pinwheel quilt and matching pillow sham that Mom hand-stitched with pink-and-blue-rosebud calico lay perfectly on her twin-sized bed. I eyed my two favorite studio shots of Kayla at age three, looking angelic in lacy ruffles and bows and a darling pageboy haircut. They hung framed on her wall with "K-A-Y-L-A" in blue letters – the same as Alisha's – suspended diagonally between them.

Suddenly I caught my breath as I caught a glimpse of the t-shirt and shorts Kayla wore the day before our accident, still crumpled on the floor. Getting home late that night, I had quickly undressed my sleeping preschooler and left her clothes in a heap as I quickly put her to bed. Now I wanted to pick them up, hold them to my face, smell her…and remember. But all I could do was look through my tears to the writing on the wall: "No Mommy Allowed."

We hadn't been home an hour, and already wounds abounded, marking not only the woodwork, but my spirit as well. Shannon and Cathie warned me, but I didn't believe them. Home had always been my sanctuary, my haven of rest. Things were always better at home. But now, home sweet home didn't seem so sweet. The life I yearned for was in sight, and completely out of reach.

Then my girls came home.

A Not So Happy Birthday

He was despised and rejected by men, a
man of sorrows, and familiar with suffering.
Like one from whom men hide their faces he
was despised, and we esteemed him not.
ISAIAH 53:3

"Happy Birthday to you! Happy birthday to you! Happy Birthday, dear Alisha…" My shy two-year-old frowned and buried her face in her hands. She hated being the center of attention in large crowds.

Phil always said toddlers' birthday parties were for moms. The invitations, decorations, guests, cake, video, pictures… He was right. Little ones are easily overwhelmed by all the people and excitement, and when the festivities linger into naptime, they get cranky. Most of them, like Alisha, would be completely satisfied with an intimate family celebration like the one we had two weeks before on her actual birthday. She enjoyed every minute, and yet, I told myself that she wanted a big celebration. Perhaps it was more accurate to say that *I* wanted a big celebration. Now I wasn't so sure.

Alisha smeared birthday cake all over her face and dress. "What a mess!" I grimaced, laughing and aching at the same time. On one hand, I rejoiced to be alive and at home to see my daughter's birthday, watching her cute little face covered in icing and chocolate cake crumbs. But on the other hand, nothing about life at home had turned out as I imagined.

Sitting in the corner, I watched my family as if through a window, unable to really be a part of all that was going on. Alisha sat on *Daddy's* lap as she tore open her gifts. My *niece* snapped photographs. And the *other women* scurried to serve cake and ice cream. Even *the neighborhood grocery store* had to make the cake. Heaven forbid! My cute teddy bear, Winnie-the-Pooh, and Mickey Mouse creations substituted by a generic rectangle with primary colored balloons.

As Alisha shoveled another forkful of cake that wasn't nearly as good as mine into her mouth, a red glob of balloon landed in her lap. I winced again and groaned under my breath. I couldn't clean her up. On second thought, maybe that was good. Red store-made icing was nearly impossible to get out of clothes.

Grandma Madalene swooped in for the rescue. She whisked Alisha's dress over her head and cleaned her face, soaking her red and white polka-dotted pinafore in cold water and color-safe bleach. Then she dressed her granddaughter in a fresh t-shirt and skort and sent her off to play before cleaning the kitchen. Madalene obviously had everything under control. *A little too much*, I thought enviously.

Phil's mom has always been an important part of our lives. I love her dearly. And I love how close she is with her grandchildren, and they with her – something I never experienced with my grandparents. But grief can cloud normal perspective. Suffice it to say, I wasn't myself. So when my mother-in-law moved in to help her son around the house and transition the girls into life at home, jealousy soon dug its ugly talons into my heart.

Honestly, I was jealous of just about everyone. My therapists, my husband, my parents, my friends… I watched *everyone* who could walk across the floor or grasp and turn a doorknob and secretly accused, *you don't have the slightest clue how blessed you are!*

Unfortunately, I felt the same toward Madalene. We needed her, and I was grateful for everything Madalene so eagerly did. But I didn't want to need her. Day after day I watched her do all that I was supposed to do as a mother and homemaker in my own home. All of the things I most wanted to do – put groceries away, cook dinner, clear the table, pick up the girls' toys, fold their laundry, give them baths – things mothers do every day and take for granted – things children need from their mothers.

Oh, and how I coveted the way the girls *needed* Madalene. I longed to pick them up as she did, to run after them at the first sound of distress as she would, to meet their needs as she could. But what hurt the most, and tainted everything else with bitterness, was watching the hugs and kisses my baby girl lavished on her.

After two weeks at home, Alisha was *still* not so fond of me. My three-month-stint away from home, and away from her, was a long time in my toddler's young life. During this critically important developmental period, she became quite attached to Grandma Madalene and was perfectly content to keep it that way.

"Mama! Mama!" Alisha called as she ran into the room.

I looked up to greet my little birthday girl only to see her at Madalene's feet. Alisha stretched her arms up.

"Mama," she said again, wanting to be held.

I thought I would lose it right then and there as the stabbing pain of rejection impaled my heart.

Sensitive to my feelings, yet helpless to alter Alisha's response, Madalene looked at me empathetically.

"Where's Mommy?" she asked playfully as she picked up her granddaughter.

Alisha shyly pointed at me, staring daggers, like she wished I would just go away again. I was not the Mommy my toddler remembered, or wanted for that matter. Just my approach or general glance in her direction sent Alisha flying to Grandma or Daddy. My big wheelchair was unfamiliar and strange to her, and my intimidating, wounded appearance was frightening. I looked like Godzilla to my little girl. I scared her. And that was more than I could bear.

Everyone tried to comfort me, explaining that Alisha's reaction was "logical and natural." Their patronizing only made me angry. *I'm not stupid*, I thought. *I know why she's doing it, but knowing why doesn't help!* Emotional pain is not always eased by understanding. And certainly logic and nature do not and can not replace our need to be loved by our children. I ached for my baby girl, plain and simple.

I was thankful I didn't altogether miss this milestone in my precious daughter's life. She was the radiant center of attention at her party as every little girl should be, and I was gratefully there to witness her big event. But as I yearned for her attention, Alisha never seemed to notice me much. I would have given anything to be her favorite gift. Yet from what I could tell, she didn't even care if I was in the room.

Oh, God, please…let her love me again!

chapter nineteen

School's in Session

*Therefore, as God's chosen people, holy and dearly
loved, clothe yourselves with compassion...*
COLOSSIANS 3:12

Kayla held my hand and skipped along as Daddy rushed me through the deserted halls. She seemed truly happy in spite of the fact that we were several minutes late to "Meet the Teacher." I was mortified. We underestimated the time it took to get me in and out of the car, and now I felt I needed a hall pass to keep from getting detention. Not at all how I pictured this moment.

As we wheeled through the doorway, Kayla's kindergarten room bulged with nervous, fidgety five-year-olds and their doting parents – and all eyes shifted to us. I kept looking forward, trying to hide my embarrassment and prayed Kayla wasn't as horrified as I. The teacher, Mrs. Truman, courteously interrupted her speech to welcome us.

"Come in, come in..." she said, and directed us to Kayla's desk. "We just got started."

Phil parked me beside the short flat-topped table and squatted his large frame onto Kayla's little red chair, like all the other parents. Kayla climbed onto Daddy's knee. Across the room I recognized a little boy from Kayla's Sunday school class. His parents waved, happily surprised to see us. I was relieved to see someone we knew.

Mrs. Truman resumed her presentation and referred to the printed materials on the desk as she explained the year's curriculum and classroom rules. Her first name, Michelle, suited her appearance better than her last. Truman brought to mind a stately older woman standing beside her presidential husband. This Mrs. Truman, however, must have been only in her late twenties. Short brown hair sweetly framed her radiant, rosy complexion. She bore the predictable glow of an expectant mother in her red and navy plaid maternity jumper as she announced her fourth child's arrival around Christmas. I wondered from the looks of her if it would be that long.

After Mrs. Truman finished her intro-to-kindergarten speech and answered every anxious question, we waited for a few moments alone. Once the other parents and children dispersed, Mrs. Truman shut the door and greeted us with eager affection, like we'd known her for years.

"I'm so glad you stayed. You must be Mom...and Dad," she said warmly, shaking my hand first and then recognizing Phil. She ignored my baggy sweats and bandages and looked straight into my eyes with appreciation. I loved her instantly. Without saying a word, she made it perfectly clear that she valued first my important role as Kayla's Mom, and refused to size me up according to my disability.

"We want you to know what has happened in Kayla's life this summer..." I began.

"Wonderful," she said, and winked, "Would it be okay if I showed Miss Kayla around first?" As she spoke, it became apparent that her kind, patient, and gentle spirit was the perfect match for our timid and sensitive little girl.

Mrs. Truman busied Kayla with exploring the various "centers" of activity in her new classroom. I studied the vivid primary-colored bulletin boards, each bursting with a cheerful welcome, and concluded, though much has changed over the years, the familiarity of an elementary schoolroom never will. Coat hooks lined the wall beneath a row of cubbies. Freshly sharpened #2 lead pencils stood like yellow soldiers, peering above a personalized teacher's mug. The green chalkboards gleamed, untouched by first attempts at simple spelling words, and black fuzzy erasers lined the chalk trays underneath, begging to get dirty. Picture books and early readers held their place in perfect alphabetical order and rainbow reams of construction paper filled the shelves.

Just as my mind floated back to my first day of kindergarten, Mrs. Truman returned, "You were saying?"

Phil and I briefly explained the emotional roller coaster of our little girl's summer. We described my injury and the miracle of my progress, even though I still had a long way to go. Mrs. Truman listened with awe. Much to our joy and relief, she expressed how she shared our faith in God and His power to still work miracles.

"I can't imagine what this has been like for you…for all of you," she said sympathetically.

"The past three months have been a bit stressful," I understated, "but Kayla has handled it all so well. She's truly been an amazing, brave little girl. Still, you may see things in her that we don't. That's why we wanted to talk to you privately."

"If I do, I will certainly let you know," Mrs. Truman promised. "My door is always open. You have my number here at school and at home," she said, referring to the stack of papers in my lap. "If there is anything I can do…"

Honestly, I was still a bit anxious to put Kayla on the bus a couple of mornings later, as are most mothers. But after meeting Mrs. Truman, I felt much better. Not only was she a capable, professional educator with over ten years' experience, she was also a concerned mother with the same ideals and values for her own young children. I couldn't have asked for anyone better qualified. And I knew my little girl would love school.

"Are you excited?" I asked Kayla at breakfast.

"Uh huh," she said, poking the last bite of cereal into her mouth. Grandma Madalene cleared the table as Kayla slid on her white canvas Mary Jane shoes and fastened the Velcro strap.

"You look absolutely gorgeous this morning!" I boasted.

Kayla had carefully chosen to wear a school-bus-yellow sleeveless romper that buttoned up the front. She kissed me on the cheek, "Thank you, Mommy!"

Daddy pinned her name, address and phone number to her white collar as the school requested and checked her backpack. Everything was there – red and blue spiral notebooks, kitty cat pocket folders, a small plastic school box with pencils, crayons, scissors... All were labeled and ready to go. My little ray of sunshine slung the metallic green backpack over her shoulders and scooted out the door.

Kayla excitedly climbed the monstrous black steps of the school bus like a trooper. At the top she turned and sweetly posed for Daddy to take a picture. From my wheelchair a few feet away, I followed her cocoa-brown ponytail past each row of kids as she made her way to her seat. If she was the slightest bit nervous, it didn't show. The only tears shed were mine, but I held them back until the huge yellow bus revved its engine and pulled away with my petite baby waving through the window.

I wasn't sad...well, maybe just a little. Mostly I was proud. I remembered how my mother wisely advised me not to wish away the hard days of Kayla's infancy. "You'll blink, and she'll start kindergarten." I took her words to heart and tried to cherish the years, although the last three months were a horribly rude interruption. Still, it all seemed to pass in the blink of an eye. And now, here I was, watching the bus take her away.

I took comfort in the knowledge that God had something remarkable planned for Kayla's life. I had no doubt. Not only had she displayed amazing courage over the last three months, her thoughtfulness astounded everyone. Phil and I knew it wasn't easy for Kayla to see her mother so helpless. It was certainly hard for her to witness the pain and endure the struggles we all faced as a family. But when my disability frustrated me to tears, my lovely daughter nobly carried on with incredible style, showering me with love as if her hugs would fix everything. In a large way, they did.

Only twice did Mrs. Truman call with concern after finding Kayla in tears. Otherwise, our daughter was happy and helpful in the classroom, the teacher said. Kayla donned compassion and wore it stunningly. She eagerly befriended other shy children who struggled with self-confidence. Kayla's kindness impressed the school's staff so much, they awarded her the first "Top Bulldog Award" of the year – the school's top honor for students displaying respect, sensitivity, and responsibility.

Possessing incredible insight for such a tender age, my five-year-old's wisdom and deep sense of compassion did not come from years of experience. They rose from within a soft heart and an unselfish spirit.

One day I felt a dose of Kayla's mercy as I edited some video footage of a concert we did three weeks prior to the accident. Phil needed the help for the new project he was working on, and I needed something to keep me occupied. It was the perfect solution, or so we thought. Wrong. Seeing the old me in motion was more than my fragile emotions could take. I tried to hide my sadness from Kayla who plopped herself on the couch nearby, wanting to watch with me. But my shoulders began to shake as sobs quickly overwhelmed me.

"Look at me!" I cried. "My hands…my hair… I'm singing…on my feet!"

With wisdom beyond her years, my little girl understood my spouts of gibberish and flung her arms around my shoulders.

"Don't worry, Mommy, you are still beautiful to me!"

This remarkable little girl amazed me with her intuition. It didn't matter to her that I couldn't fix my hair. She wasn't bothered when most days I didn't have the energy to apply make-up. She'd still crawl into my lap and snuggle, careful to avoid "Mama's ouchies." Kayla didn't love me for how I looked or what I could do for her; she loved me for who I was…her mama.

School was in session. Daily, I released my child into the big wide world, wondering what she would learn and how she would fare. Yet it was I who became the student. My kindergartner taught unconditional love by example. She saw past the scars, and tutored me to do the same as she willingly modeled patience and persistence. Kayla may have been a first-time student in the world's eyes. But in mine, she became a first-class teacher with the Master's degree in compassion.

At His Feet

Consider it pure joy, my brothers, whenever you
face trials of many kinds, because you know that
the testing of your faith develops perseverance.
Perseverance must finish its work so that you may
be mature and complete, not lacking anything.

JAMES 1:2-4

"OK, lift," Phil said, ready to slide my britches over my rear as I lay like a lump on the bed.

"Very funny," I said.

"No, really. I want you to try."

With every ounce of energy in me, I tried to raise my hips. I took in a deep breath, squinted my eyes shut, grunted, and pushed. But when I let my breath out and opened my eyes, Phil hadn't moved and neither had I.

"Go ahead, anytime," he teased.

"That is *not funny!*" I whined as a slight smile curled my lips. Phil rolled me side to side, inching my sweat pants up to my waist.

Our morning routine – cathing, showering, medicating, bandaging, dressing, and eating – took a minimum of three hours, often nearly four. Frustrating as it was, I enjoyed Phil's undivided attention. We did our best to make light of the situation, sometimes more successfully than other times.

When the care was complete, Phil was off to work and perform other household chores. I was exhausted...bored, depressed, and alone, again. I resisted the desire to nap. I wouldn't sleep at night if I slept all day, so I looked for another way – any way – to occupy my mind and distract myself. Reading didn't work. Weakness made the whole process just plain miserable. Turning the pages was an irritating struggle with limp fingers, and although I was now free of the neck brace, wearing it for three months weakened my muscles. Combined with the neurological weakness in my arms, holding a book close enough to read comfortably wore me out by the end of the first page. After a few minutes of trying, the ache in my neck and shoulders turned a good book into a nuisance.

TV wasn't much fun without company, and I didn't want the kids watching it all afternoon. Besides, operating the remote was impossible unless perfectly placed in my lap. I hated to ask for help. I didn't want to be a burden. Phil couldn't be interrupted every five minutes, and Madalene had better things to do than babysit my helpless, sorry self.

Actually, excuses like these masked the honest truth. I hated to ask for help, because much like my extremely stubborn toddler, I wanted to do it all myself. I discovered that little apple didn't fall too far from this tree. When I needed help, I often sat for what seemed like hours until someone happened by. Relentless pride ruled my life and stole my joy, dwindling life to mere existence and turning my home into what felt like a prison.

With each passing day, my inabilities seemed to grow and aggravation paralleled their ascent. It took so much time, forethought, and energy to get me ready to leave the house, we usually chose not to go. If it required getting up before dawn, like going to church on Sunday – forget it.

If we did decide to venture out, we had to consider my cathing schedule. Every four hours I needed a co-ed appropriate place where I could comfortably and sanitarily lay down for Phil to do the honors. And depending on what I drank and how much, we may have been pressed to find accommodations quickly. Unless we visited someone at home, such a place didn't exist. So we had to carefully plan how long we would be gone, factoring in travel time, and *stick to the schedule.* The latter was the hardest part.

On one occasion, not long after my homecoming, we decided I needed a new recliner – something easy for Phil to transfer me in and out of that would be comfortable. I was thrilled for the opportunity to get out of the house to shop! It had been so long...

We all enjoyed the diversion so much that we lost track of time. Moments faded to hours much too quickly, and as we narrowed our selection, I felt the early warning signs that our time was short. I glanced at my watch. Our time wasn't short, it was *up*! We should have already been home, yet we still had more than a thirty-minute drive ahead.

Much to my amazement and discomfort, we made it home by the grace of God without incident. I just didn't make it inside the house. Oh, what a mess!

"I'm so sorry!" I wailed, embarrassed to tears.

"It's okay," Phil comforted. Madalene hurried the girls inside. She knew how I hated for them to see me like this. "At least we're in the garage," he said, and then mused, "Park yourself over the drain. It's no big deal."

But it was a huge deal to me.

I decided then and there that getting out simply wasn't worth it. Rehab was my only safe and consistent connection to the outside world. It gave me something to do, a place to belong, and people who could understand and handle the demands and limitations of my body. It gave me an opportunity to move beyond the mundane monotony of sitting in silence and watching painfully as someone else cleaned my house and took care of my family. It gave me a chance to work toward re-claiming my life.

In September, the insurance company cut down my daily therapy to only three days a week. I panicked. I had only been an outpatient for two weeks, and from where I sat, nothing had changed in that brief span. Shannon stood beside my case manager, Charlotte, as she broke the news.

"What? What do they mean I *no longer need* therapy every day?" I asked in shock.

"The medical director at the insurance company has reviewed

your progress, and thinks you are ready," Charlotte said.

"How does he know? He isn't here. He isn't me! How am I supposed to get stronger without therapy every day? I've got news for him, I'm not ready!"

Their cut-backs cut me to the core. Some "director," whoever he was, didn't think my independence was worth the money it took to reclaim it. I was crushed.

"Pam, you'll be fine," Shannon said. "I admit, this isn't ideal, but you are going to need therapy for a long time. We have a better chance of extending the big picture by going along with this."

I respected Shannon and trusted her advice, so I calmed down and rolled with the decision, even though I didn't like it one bit.

Life moved on...and it was leaving without me. More and more, I found myself incarcerated at home. Besides therapy, an occasional quick mid-day jaunt to the post office and bank with Phil was my only reprieve.

Just when I thought no one could possibly understand, I received a letter from my neighbor, Vicki. Months before, Vicki discovered she suffered from an extremely rare disorder. Without warning, her heart rate accelerates to dangerously high levels; her body kicks into "fight or flight" as if panicked. Lying flat on her back and waiting for her body to relax is the only way to prevent cardiac arrest.

Vicki gradually learned to identify the internal signals that warn of impending attacks, but as the mysterious ailment progressed, her life became extremely restricted. Many days she could only stand or sit upright for a total of three hours. Bravely my neighbor resolved to take her condition in stride. Setting aside her pride, she chose to focus on what she could do, rather than what she couldn't.

In her letter, Vicki described how Phil's song, "Martha," ministered to her through her illness. The lyrics are based on Luke 10:38-42: When Martha prepares dinner for Jesus and His disciples, she becomes frustrated with her sister, Mary, who chooses to sit and listen to Jesus rather than help in the kitchen. As she spills her annoyance before the entire crowd, Jesus answers her,

Martha, Martha, you worry about many things…
but sometimes you've got to let it go.
Just take a little lesson from Mary.
Child, she knows what matters most.[1]

Jesus' confrontation with a harried Martha sounded a lot like Vicki's advice to me now.

I know there are some moments when you get a
little disappointed with the circumstances you're in…

I rolled my eyes and nodded. *What an understatement*, I thought. Suddenly I envisioned God's gentle, yet firm, hands on each side of my face, turning it toward His. *Be still and listen*, echoed quietly in my soul.

About a year after my illness, when I was
complaining about my circumstances and telling
God how I could do so much more for Him if I were
well again, He told me something that has helped
me. He spoke in such a soft voice as He said, 'Can't
you be happy being Mary for awhile instead of being
Martha?'
   You see, I loved being 'Martha', and I don't think
Martha was doing wrong. Somebody needs to do all
these things, right?!!

"Yes!" I wanted to scream. "And it should be me!" What a relief to finally be understood…

But sitting at Jesus' feet and learning from
Him and about Him is so needed, so wonderful.
Sometimes we get so busy we have no time to just
'be' with Him. Now I'm never busy.

My "Martha" stirred obstinately inside of me. Then I read…

You know, I can't wait to hear the new songs that
come from the walk that you're on with God now.
It will truly be heavenly inspired. Keep up the good
work. God is using you to reach people in a whole
new way. The world is watching you and learning
volumes...

My stubborn pride melted, and the war within me paused. *The world is watching,* I read again. What did they see? A depressed and scared little girl who demanded her own way? What insight could they possibly glean from me? All at once I felt the presence of Almighty God surrounding me, penetrating the darkest caverns of my heart. *It is time to grow up. It is time to be Mary,* He said. *I have chosen you to teach the world what I so desperately want to teach you.*

Fear, dread, and depression abruptly retreated, their suffocating weight lifted from my heart. I felt privileged to sit at the Master's feet and listen to His instruction, even if I never learned why this had to happen. Perhaps it took these drastic measures for God to get my attention. Or maybe there was no other way to impart the wisdom I needed to pass along.

Pondering Vicki's counsel produced an honest desire to focus, listen, and learn. My God was faithful, this I knew. I had no idea what He had in store, but I was confident it was something good. And maybe, just maybe joy would return.

I set all of the pre-opened mail that was in my lap on the dining room table, except for Vicki's letter. With a surge of strength, I pushed my wheelchair a couple of feet across the plush carpet to the kitchen linoleum and easily propelled myself to the top of the basement stairs. I called for Phil, and he poked his head around the doorway at the bottom of the steps.

"Do you need something?" he asked eagerly.

"Yes, actually, I do…I need to share this amazing letter…"

1 *"Martha" written by Phil Morgan. ©1999 Jammin' Gentile Music, BMI. Used by permission. From the Jubalee Music CD "Phil & Pam Morgan - What Matters Most"*

Thirsting for Comfort

And be sure of this: I am with
you always, even to the end of the age.
MATTHEW 28:20 (NLT)

"This place gives me the creeps," I said, shuddering as Phil wheeled me into the waiting room of my neurosurgeon's office.

"Why?"

"I'm not quite sure, but I always dread coming here."

"I think I know what you mean," Phil said. "Dr. Coufal is a great doctor, but his expectations are not very optimistic. I know he doesn't intend to squash our hopes and ruin our day, but his medical view of reality sure does the trick."

He was right. I valued Dr. Coufal's care and skill, but he didn't anticipate a miracle. Then again, I had yet to meet a doctor who did.

"Well, we've got something exciting to show him this time," I said hopefully. "Maybe he'll change his tune."

As we waited for the nurse to call my name, oppression bore down, but Phil and I grew increasingly excited to show off for Dr. Coufal. Nothing was better than watching a medical doctor encounter the unexpected. We hadn't seen him for two months, and much had happened since then.

149

The nurse finally called us back and I beamed as Dr. Coufal greeted us.

Not yet able to use my right leg, I kicked my left. Dr. Coufal sat dumbfounded as I contracted my quadricep at will, repeating the action over and over.

"This is far beyond what I ever expected, Pam," he said. "It is absolutely phenomenal progress!"

Phil and I exchanged controlled, elated glances.

"I still say I'm going to walk back in here someday."

"Well, I have to tell you…this could plateau at any time. This may be all the return you incur."

I wanted to ask Dr. Coufal if he was a believer, if he knew the same Jesus Christ I knew, who died in our place, yet rose again and still works miracles. But I didn't. I was afraid. Perhaps I feared the doctor whom I respected would reject my faith, implying it was silly, and merely a means of denying my situation. Dr. Coufal would have never said exactly that, yet I imagined seeing it in his eyes, hearing it in his tone. I chose to remain quiet, keeping to myself what I knew to be the work of my God.

Giving way to fear had dreadful repercussions. I stewed over Dr. Coufal's warning and became an easy target once again for doubt and grief. My progress was slow and erratic, much more so than I had envisioned. What if the doctor was right? What if I didn't get any more return?

I thought of my sister's three-year battle with cancer. All that time our family prayed for Denise's healing and comfort. Yet God seemed silent. During the final stages of her illness, I "encouraged" her with Paul's words in his second letter to the Corinthians, although I didn't fully understand it myself. *"…there was given me a thorn in my flesh, a messenger of Satan, to torment me. Three times I pleaded with the Lord to take it away from me. But He said to me, 'My grace is sufficient for you, for My power is made perfect in weakness.'"* (12:7-9)

Paul had to pray three times for relief before God answered. I wondered in the scope of time how long the delay actually was. A day? A week? A month? Scripture doesn't say. I prayed every night for God to remove my "thorn," yet every morning I was disappointed. If Paul had to wait it out, how did God's silence make him feel? And when Paul finally did get an answer, how did he feel when God essentially said, "No!"? Did he wrestle with Psalm 37:4 - "*Delight yourself in the LORD and he will give you the desires of your heart*"? I did. I reminded God of this promise every night, hoping that I would awake completely healed.

One of our faithful, praying supporters sent me the book, *You Gotta Keep Dancin'*, by Tim Hansel, as encouragement. The story was about the author's experience with pain after a tragic mountain-climbing accident. Out of love and respect for the dear lady who sent it, I started to read Hansel's book. I made it to the sixth chapter. But a couple of pages later, I put it down and not because of physical pain. I just couldn't read anymore. The chapter title alone made me cringe – "Choose Joy." Right away Hansel described the difference between joy and happiness. He said happiness is from the root word "*happening, suggesting [it] is based on something happening to us. Joy, on the other hand, is something which defies circumstances and occurs in spite of difficult situations. Whereas happiness is a feeling, joy is an attitude. A posture. A place. As Paul Sailhamer says, 'Joy is that deep settled confidence that God is in control of every area of my life.'*" [1]

I have since finished the entire book and recommend it highly, but at that point of my journey, I couldn't get past page 55. Hansel wrote, "*At any moment in life, we have at least two options, and one of them is to choose an attitude of gratitude, a posture of grace, and a commitment to joy.*" I didn't disagree with everything Hansel said, but I wasn't sure joy was within my reach. I thought that choosing my daily attitude in spite of how I felt was like selecting an outfit to wear that wasn't in my closet.

I *was* confident God held my life in His grasp. But that was the point. My life was in God's grasp, not mine. Thinking of Job's suffering and knowing that the Almighty's ways weren't always my ways, I began to worry. The desire of my heart was to walk, yet in God's silence to my prayers, I wondered if Dr. Coufal's pessimistic projections were God's choice for my life. If so, how was I supposed to be joyful about that?

Visiting pastors and friends offered biblical answers that brought little comfort. *"And we know that in all things God works for the good of those who love Him, who have been called according to His purpose,"* (Romans 8:28) was a popular one. How could this be for my good? If this was God's idea of good, I wasn't sure I wanted to be called.

The more I thought about Scripture's answers, the more disturbed I became. *Something must be wrong with me,* I thought. Whatever it was, I felt terrible. I argued, *If this is your call, God, you've got the wrong person. I can't do this. And frankly, I don't want to do this. Put me back the way I was.*

The silence continued. Why didn't God answer? Where was He?

What bothered me most was loneliness. From childhood, I learned that Jesus left Heaven's splendor and stepped inside the skin of a common man so that He could understand our lives.

> *For we do not have a high priest who is unable to*
> *sympathize with our weaknesses, but we have one*
> *who has been tempted in every way, just as we*
> *are — yet was without sin.* - **HEBREWS 4:15**

I always drew strength from this promise. I wanted to believe Jesus identified with my distress more than anyone. Certainly nothing could compare to the agony of crucifixion. I reminded myself of that over and over. And yet, something still gnawed away at my soul. Although Jesus healed the lame many times, not once in Scripture was He ever bound to a wheelchair. It hurt to think that God would subject me to something He had never experienced, and perhaps wasn't willing to bear.

One evening I sat in the kitchen, watching Madalene and Phil clean up after dinner. Fatigued after a long, rough day in therapy, my neck and shoulders ached. I stared at the refrigerator and longed for a cold drink. Under the blazing desire to get it myself, frustration mushroomed once again. I couldn't begin to reach the glasses in the cupboard. Nor could my floppy fingers open the refrigerator door, hold a pitcher, or pour a drink.

Just then, Alisha zipped into the room and over to the refrigerator. Her strong little fingers clutched the handle, pulled it open, and grabbed her tippy cup of milk. As the door slammed shut behind her, I felt the enemy taunting me, "Look what she can do... and you can't!"

Devastated, I sobbed. Enough was enough. "Jesus, you can't possibly understand what this feels like!" I cried. "I can't even get myself a drink of water!"

All at once, the silence broke. In my mind I heard my Savior's voice cry, "I thirst." His words echoed as I pictured Him hanging on the cross, bound by nails, writhing in unimaginable agony... and parched as the dry wind blew dust in His face. Suddenly I was overwhelmed as I realized that Christ was unable to get Himself anything to drink. In a way, He was paralyzed to the cross. But not by the nails; legions of angels would have loved to deliver Him, or at the very least, gotten Him a drink of water if only He had said the word. No...Jesus willingly clung to the cross, because *He loved me.* Jesus chose the pain, first and foremost because His sacrifice was the only way I could spend eternity with Him. But my future wasn't all He had on His mind. I believed that as He hung crucified, the Messiah of the world saw me two thousand years later, sitting in a wheelchair, desperate to know that He had been there, too.

When anxiety was great within me, your consolation brought joy to my soul. - **PSALMS 94:19**

The ancient psalmist's words were now my own. Tears streamed down my face and dropped into my lap, but not as a bitter overflow of loneliness as before. My Savior's voice transcended my circumstances, and rooted amazing, inexpressible, unreasonable, and undeniable joy deep in my heart. In the midst of my living nightmare, Jesus was there. I relaxed in His embrace, knowing He understood exactly how I felt.

Joy, or gladness, is what man craves and is set upon finding; and he does find it when he finds God, and only then. - **CONCISE BIBLE DICTIONARY, P. 2715**

1 Hansel, Tim. *You Gotta Keep Dancin',* p. 53, David C. Cook Publishing, Elgin, IL, copyright 1985.

chapter twenty-two

By My Side

Husbands, love your wives, just as Christ
loved the church and gave Himself up for her.
EPHESIANS 5:25

I had big news – absolutely huge – and as Mom and Dad taxied me home from rehab, I couldn't wait to tell Phil. Daddy usually drove too fast for my taste, swinging around curves at speeds that nearly tipped me over in my seat. But today, of all days, he eased his pace. I should have been relieved; instead, I was annoyed.

Finally, we rounded the corner to our house. Kayla peddled her pink Barbie bicycle in large loops on the driveway. Phil watched her from the shade of our scarlet pin oak, lounging in an old lawn chair. Its frayed green mesh straps and rickety metal frame reminded me of autumn camping trips as a kid.

I tried to think about those fun weekend getaways as a means of distraction while Phil transferred me from Mom and Dad's Cadillac into my wheelchair. Smoky campfires, gooey marshmallows charred on a stick, Herman, the hungry basset hound, following every move, waiting with bated breath for one to drop… A smile crept across my lips at the thought of that silly dog.

"You seem happy," Phil said. "What's up?"

"Oh, nothing," I said, holding back my excitement. The

moment had to be perfect before I spilled the news.

Kayla greeted me with a hug and kiss. Surely she felt my heart pounding in my chest.

"Hi Sweetheart, how was your day?"

"Good," she said, and took off on her bike once again, too busy to share any more details at the moment.

I waved goodbye to Mom and Dad, smiling through the windshield. I was thankful they kept my secret. Phil moved his lawn chair to the top of the driveway and parked me next to it. As he sat, my husband interlaced my limp fingers with his, and held them tight against his knuckles with his other hand. At that moment, no other place in the world could be more perfect.

"Where's Alisha?"

"Inside with Grandma," Phil said.

I've got you all to myself, I thought and asked, "So…how was *your* day?"

I listened patiently as Phil recapped his latest undertakings. I took in a deep breath of patience and thanked God for him. What a miracle he was in my life. If things had gone my way fifteen years ago… I shuddered just thinking about it.

———⧸∾∾⧹———

Phil and I met as seniors in high school. As part of the Kansas City All-Metro Choir, we sang outside Crown Center for the lighting of the Mayor's Christmas tree the day after Thanksgiving. My thin flannel-lined insignia jacket didn't begin to shelter me from the freezing temperatures and cutting wind that night, but I barely noticed. Instead, this giddy alto anticipated her first date with a cute tenor I met during rehearsals. But it wasn't Phil. I had a date with John, one of his best friends. I didn't meet Phil until John introduced him as our chauffeur. John's little red sports car was an accident waiting to happen in the snow and ice, but instead of breaking our date, John convinced Phil to cart us around in his 1978 two-tone-green Chevy van. It seemed a little odd, but I agreed.

At John's house later that evening, Phil slid me his business card. *What in the world?* I thought. Most teenagers didn't walk around carrying business cards. But then again, a burger flipper at the local fast food chain didn't necessarily need one.

"If you need to talk about John," he whispered, "just call."

I glanced down at the little white card in my hand. In blue printing, it read,

Phil Morgan
Piano and Vocals - Composing and Arranging
Solo Performance - Any Occasion

His address and phone number were listed at the bottom. I had no idea what Phil was talking about, but I was intrigued. No other seventeen-year-old I knew ventured into entrepreneurial music. I slid the card into my coat pocket.

A couple of weeks later, the motivation behind Phil's comment came to light as I discovered the truth about my cute new boyfriend. Phil and John attended Raytown High School, arch rival to my alma mater in the south part of town. On Sunday afternoon, I had another date with John after their choir's annual Christmas concert.

The choir sang a beautiful Christmas composition to close the concert that I had never heard before. Once the last note trailed off and the director dropped his arms, the audience roared with whistles and applause. The director bowed and then motioned for Phil to come forward.

"In case you are wondering, this young man, Phil Morgan, wrote that last piece," he announced.

My jaw dropped. *Who is this guy?*

When the ovation finally died down, I made my way to the foyer and found a bench to warm while John turned in his choir robe. Phil greeted a swarm of people nearby, seeking to commend his work. He glanced my way and smiled. I waved and mouthed, "Awesome!"

The auditorium cleared within ten minutes, and I began to fidget. *Where is John?* I checked my watch. What was taking so long?

The last handful of people lingered in the foyer around Phil. He excused himself and approached the bench where I sat...still waiting.

"Hi, Pam," Phil said and sat beside me, his voice somewhat apprehensive. "John wanted me to tell you his aunt died..." He sighed. "But I can't. I have to be honest. You are too nice to be one of John's girls."

I was stunned. Already guessing what was about to come next, I braced myself.

"The truth is...John has another date. He double-booked with number three, or maybe with number four...I'm not sure. Anyway, he ducked out the back door to meet her."

"What number am I?" I snapped.

"I...don't...really...know," Phil stammered. "All I know is John has always dated lots of girls at a time, and they're all from different high schools. None of them know about the others... until now."

I couldn't believe it. I was heartbroken...and humiliated.

Phil obviously hated the task his friend thrust upon him, so as a consolation for both of us, he offered to buy me a Coke at Fuddruckers. It didn't take much convincing for me to give in.

Clad in a black tuxedo, Phil took my arm and escorted me across the slick parking lot. He chose a private high-top table for two, and held my chair as I situated myself in the tall seat. Four fascinating hours flew by with this talented mystery man, who possessed the clearest blue eyes I had ever seen. Several refills, stories, and even the beginning of a song later, our relationship had begun. I was star-struck, and yet perfectly at ease.

Phil openly admits he fell in love that night at Fuddruckers. I, on the other hand, refused to jump into romance again. Truth be known, Phil's chivalrous behavior won my protective father over first. It impressed Daddy that Phil opened every door, held my chair, and thanked Mom for her home-cooked meals. When Phil had a dozen red roses delivered to school for my eighteenth birthday, Dad was convinced Phil was the one worthy of winning his little girl's heart.

"That Phil is one good lookin' guy...," Daddy prompted as I set the arranged roses on the kitchen table.

"You go out with him then!" I teased stubbornly.

I didn't want to be rushed, especially when it came to getting serious with someone – a quality I hope my daughters inherit. Still, Phil's charm and Dad's approval gradually opened my eyes to the possibility of something more serious. I felt like a queen whenever Phil and I were together.

By prom, he was more than my friend, he was my date. Soon I couldn't imagine my life without him, and except for a few months of insanity during college, I have adored him ever since.

We married at my home church, Peace Lutheran, in Kansas City, Missouri, on October 20, 1990. My childhood pastor, Rev. John Schmid, performed the ceremony, reading Genesis 2:23-24. *"The man said, 'This is now bone of my bones and flesh of my flesh; she shall be called "woman," for she was taken out of man.' For this reason a man will leave his father and mother and be united with his wife, and they will become one flesh."*

Nine years later, Phil stood by my side in the Intensive Care Unit, his eyes filled with tears. "I'm so glad you are still my wife," he said. "This is not just your injury. This is our injury. We will make it through this *together* with God's help."

All through my hospitalization and in-patient rehab, nurses applauded Phil's tenacity. "You've got a gem in that guy," they said. "Most husbands would have walked out by now. It happens all the time. It's rare for a man to stay by a woman's side when something like this happens."

Phil stuck like glue. *"For better or for worse, in sickness and in health, as long as we both shall live."* Committed to his vows, my husband jumped in with both feet to learn the ins and outs of caring for his quadriplegic wife.

During the most degrading moments, his humor sheltered my dignity and saved my sanity. I love his dry, quick wit. I anticipate it. I depend on it. I tend to be more serious and wallow in self-pity when I'm miserable or humiliated. But the man I married inevitably finds a way to make even the most disgusting chores funny.

Evacuating my bowel was the perfect example. Phil's fifth-grade humor transformed the most demeaning daily chore into comedic entertainment. His creative string of one-liners prohibited disgrace or depression. I can still see it: after a lift and heave to the bedside commode, Phil placed a bed pan on the floor underneath my bottom, and then sprawled on the floor for a better view – much like an oil change. With a touch of drama, he snapped a rubber glove in place, applied a glob of KY, and proclaimed, "I've got you wrapped around my finger."

Never in our wildest dreams did either of us ever imagine a moment like this as we stood at the altar nearly ten years before. Here we were – sharing our oneness – flesh, bone, poop and all. My husband's whimsical wit overpowered the filth and stench with the lovely aroma of silliness and indescribable tenderness. We laughed, and I loved him more than ever.

I wish I could say we made light of such things every day, that we bravely fought the battle with unwavering optimism to make the best of it all. But that would be a lie.

Adjusting to a dramatic life-changing injury is arduous – physically and emotionally – for everyone involved, especially for a primary care-giver who is also the spouse. So much rests on their shoulders. Phil's responsibilities more than doubled. Not only did he have to fill my role as well as his own, he became my full-time nurse. Unending demands day-in and day-out wore him down. A home healthcare-giver was not covered by insurance, and way beyond our unemployed-at-the-moment budget, so Phil was it. He never got a break. Twenty-four/seven, Phil's duties pressed in from all sides – nurse, Dad, Mom, housekeeper, counselor.

On weekends, he felt obligated to continue our ministry, so Phil resumed the tour dates already booked within one hundred miles from home. Up to this point, our bills were paid through gracious donations from well-wishing supporters. Yet my husband found it stressful to constantly camp on the receiving end of charity. He wanted to give something back in return. So in addition to the domestic burden he carried during the week, ministry and travel tagged along on the weekends.

Exhaustion set in. I saw it in his face, heard it in his voice, and felt it in his actions. Phil was often overwhelmed, and soon his tender, understanding side faded. His humor turned sarcastic and hurtful. My husband carried out his commitments and took care of his responsibilities, but his joy shriveled away. What ripped me up inside was the constant realization that I was the source of his load.

One afternoon in September, Brenda and Alan Black stopped by to visit. In the safety and confidence of our dear friends, Phil unloaded his stress. He described the tug-of-war pulling his heart between the music ministry and his family responsibilities. He was torn, unsure of how to balance the two things he felt called to do.

"There is a season for everything," Brenda said. "For now, your family is your ministry. God has called you to stay home and take care of them."

"That's not the ministry I want," he said bluntly.

His comment devastated me. It had nothing to do with how he felt about me, yet I convinced myself that it did. I thought my husband felt trapped, and surely his integrity and commitment to our wedding vows were all that kept him around. After all, who could love someone like me? How could anyone who saw what he had to see find me attractive?

Phil demonstrated love in the sacrifices he made to take care of me and our household. Yet something was missing. Knowing you are loved is one thing, but feeling loved is altogether different. I longed for our pre-accident intimacy. I longed for Phil to hold me like he used to. I missed watching a movie after the girls went to bed, snuggling close to him on the sofa. But the seat of our couch rested a foot off the ground, and lifting me back into the wheelchair was like hauling a refrigerator up Mt. Everest, especially with an injured collarbone.

At first, romance took priority when I came home. But getting close was difficult to say the least. Both of us had left shoulder injuries, so rolling toward each other in bed was impossible. At first it was fun to be creative, but that took time and Phil's nights were short enough. My bladder already woke him every two to four hours when "the urge" struck. If I didn't rouse him quickly enough, I wet the bed, turning a typical ten minute routine into at least forty-five. Rest became Phil's top priority. Romance slid way down the list.

It's no wonder. My mood usually didn't help. It certainly didn't invite intimacy. I hated my helplessness – unable to get my daughters a drink, mop up a mess, change a diaper. I loathed my incapacity – powerless to clear clutter in my path, throw in a load of laundry, or prepare dinner for my family. I absolutely despised my inability to slide my socks on, pull my pants up, or wipe my own bottom. But more than anything, I hated to show how lousy I was at coping to anyone besides Phil. I felt uncomfortable venting my grief in front of Madalene and the girls, so I held it back until Phil and I were alone at night.

According to my nurses, when heat rises to unbearable degrees, most people flee the inferno. It's a miracle Phil stayed, especially with as much kindling as I piled onto the flame. For weeks, I released my grief every night, wearing him out emotionally and spiritually, as well as physically. It was too much. I cried at the slightest spark of Phil's attitude, but water didn't extinguish this fire. My tear-saturated face only fueled his smoldering weariness.

"I need you to be happy for a change," Phil said, exhausted and frustrated.

"I agree. That would be nice!" I retorted before blowing up and accusing my beloved of not understanding *my* life. Then I hated myself for attacking the man I longed to hold.

In spite of my intense depression and tearful outbursts that made us both miserable, Phil stayed. My husband believed that what didn't kill us would surely strengthen us. Phil promised to hang in there *"as long as we both shall live,"* and he meant it.

Now as my hubby sat by my side in the driveway, immense gratitude came over me for the man I nearly rejected in the beginning and nearly drove away during the last several weeks. Dusk settled on that cool day of changing color as my sweetheart's day-in-review wound to a close. I had tried my best to hang on every word and fully absorb the moment.

A soft breeze ruffled our hair, tattling of autumn's arrival. But unlike changing leaves that offer a sneak peek of fall's vivid hues, some momentous events come unheralded.

"Guess what I did today?"

More Than We Can Imagine

*Now to him who is able to do immeasurably
more than all we ask or imagine...*

EPHESIANS 3:20

Even in the fading light of a sinking October sun, Phil's face shone with expectation at my simple question. Instantly he read my eager smile, and his eyes welled with tears. Without a word, those watery baby-blues told me he knew what I was about to say as if he had witnessed it himself. Still, I wanted him to know every sparkling detail, even if he already knew the outcome.

Earlier that morning, Mom and Dad arrived to haul me to therapy. Before heading out the door, Phil kissed me goodbye. "Have a *great* day," he said. How prophetic.

Dad wheeled me to the driveway and positioned my chair in the angle of the open car door, ready to help me transfer into the front seat. So far, it was just another routine day, until I motioned for Dad to wait. I wanted to try something new.

"Mom, hand me the sliding board."

Mom passed me the shiny oak sliding board my nephew crafted for me. Clumsily I managed to fumble the flat piece of heavy wood into place – one end on the car seat, and the other wedged under my left bottom cheek. Over the last several weeks, I slaved in therapy to strengthen my upper body so that I could transfer myself. Now was the moment of truth...

"Let me help you," Dad said, standing guard with outstretched arms.

"No, Dad. Remember? You're not supposed to help unless I ask you to – therapist's orders."

Dad stuffed his hands in his pockets and backed up a couple of steps. "Okay..." Dad obliged his stubborn daughter, but his familiar chuckle said he wasn't convinced it was a wise idea.

Slowly I pushed and scooted my bony behind across the makeshift bridge to the leather seat. Then with an arm under each knee I lifted my legs, one at a time, into the car. I slipped my palm behind the seatbelt buckle and pulled it across my chest, and after a few more seconds of fumbling, the buckle clicked into place.

"I made it!" I said, panting. My parents applauded like their toddler had just taken her first step. Phil's sweet send-off was already coming to pass. And in next to no time, I discovered this was just the beginning.

As soon as I arrived at the gym, I felt like pushing the envelope again. I wanted to see what else I could do. Many patients transferred themselves without a sliding board, so I wheeled myself over to a vacant mat and parked myself flush alongside. Imitating the steps Shannon took every day, I popped the lever that removed my footrests, placed my feet flat on the floor, and released my armrest – paving a clear path to the mat. With a couple of ambitious shoves, I lifted myself up and over until I sat squarely on the mat.

Just then, Shannon sauntered my way.

"Did you see that?"

Shannon nodded with a knowing smile. "Great! You see? All those heavy repetitions pushing weights are paying off!"

Suddenly the sound of ripping Velcro caught my attention as Shannon pried apart the straps on a hinged metal contraption.

"What's that?"

"A leg brace," she said, matter-of-factly. "Transfer yourself back into your chair, and meet me at the parallel bars."

"For what?"

I was stunned. Only people who could walk used the parallel bars.

"We've been strengthening that left leg. It's time to put it to the test."

Joy, doubt, and fear simultaneously exploded inside of me. I didn't think anyone in the medical field truly believed I would walk again. And at this first sign of the contrary, I was the one left wondering. Did I believe it? Was I strong enough? What if I wasn't? What if I fell? Adrenaline surged through my veins. In record time I transferred myself back into the chair and chased her – racing my wheels over the tile floors.

"Shannon, are you sure?" I said, stopping halfway there. "I mean, I don't know. I don't think I'm ready."

"We'll never know unless we try," she said.

"I don't know..."

"Listen to you, Scaredy Cat! Isn't this what you want? Isn't this what you've worked and waited for all this time?"

"Well, yes..." I said, hesitantly.

"Then get over here!"

Veronica, a comical Hispanic PT assistant, snuck up behind me and pushed me between the bars.

"You go, girl!" she said. "And don't give Channon no chit!"

"Hey! Watch your language!" I chastised.

Veronica slapped her fingers over her lips in apology. She always made me laugh. This pint-sized fireball loved her job, loved the patients, and loved to give Shannon a hard time.

"Veronica will follow with your chair and hold it steady in case you suddenly need to sit," Shannon said. She motioned for Amy, her assistant, who often subbed for Shannon, to come and help.

The four of us had become good friends over the past several months. Monotonous repetitions of leg lifts and bicep curls provided plenty of opportunities for getting to know each other. Every Monday we caught up on weekend activities. Shannon and her husband, Frank, usually stayed close to home with their toddler, Mallory. Amy wasn't sure she was ready for kids. Instead, she and her aspiring-pilot husband, Kevin, took their yellow lab and golden retriever and flew their private plane to their houseboat on the Lake of the Ozarks. Veronica always had stories to tell and advice to seek about her trying teenagers. I trusted these women. And although I had never met their families, I felt I knew them.

Shannon strapped the brace securely around my right leg and locked the knee joint in place.

"This will support your weak leg," she said. "I'm going to lift you up, and I'll guard your unbraced knee with mine to keep it from buckling. I want you to do most of the work. Use that new strength you just showed me to push yourself into place. I won't let you go, so don't be afraid. OK?"

I nodded, but was terrified.

"Are you ready?"

I hesitated, and then nodded again. The busy gym hushed. Everyone seemed to hold their breath.

Shannon pulled me forward and Amy held me steady – boosting as necessary – to help me lift and push my body weight upright on the metal bars.

"C'mon, don't make your upper body do all the work! Use that leg!" Shannon coached.

Before I knew it, there I was. My arms braced, legs locked... standing.

"Good! Good!" Shannon said. "How do you feel?"

Oh, what a question! I had waited four months for this moment. Momentary elation coursed through my body and threatened to knock me off balance.

"Whoa," Shannon said, tightening her hold on my gait belt and bracing her body against mine. "I got you...OK...there you go... now, how do you feel?"

"You're short!" I blurted.

Shannon laughed. "No, you're tall!"

She stood only two inches shorter than my five-feet-nine-inch frame, but I seemed to tower over her. Suddenly, terror gripped me.

"It's a long way down...," I said.

"It only seems that way after looking at the world from a seated position for so long. Just look straight ahead. When you're ready, we'll take a step."

Mustering my nerve, I basked for a few seconds in the feeling of intense relief. One hundred forty pounds of weight on my legs for the first time in months felt somewhat like stretching out after riding for hours in the cramped backseat of a Volkswagen bug. Or so I imagined.

"OK..." I said, "...I'm ready."

"Slide both hands forward on the bars and transfer all your weight to the right," Shannon coached.

I panicked.

"But I can't feel my right leg! It won't hold me..."

"Trust me, we won't let you fall," Shannon said. "The brace is locked. It won't buckle underneath you; use your arms to support yourself."

With a little cry, I held my breath and pushed myself forward over what felt like nothing to me. Shannon was right. The brace held.

"Good! Now kick out your left leg, and take a step."

Quickly and clumsily I threw out my heavy left foot and shifted my weight. As I stepped forward, my leg muscles instinctively contracted under my weight, remembering exactly what to do. It felt so good.

Shannon, Amy, and Veronica shouted a chorus of praise, "You did it! Good job! Way to go! Good for you!"

"How do you feel now?" Shannon said.

All I could think about was holding myself up. My arms began to tremble.

"I don't know..." I gasped, "Can I sit?"

It felt kind of strange to ask that question. In my dreams, walking would be easy when I finally could. I would stand, walk, jump, and run for hours on end. But as Shannon eased me down, the familiar security of my trusty wheelchair was a relief.

Virginia, the mother of the young man with a brain injury who roomed next door to me, instantly rushed to my side after watching the whole thing from the hallway behind me. Virginia had become like family. Over the last several months, we shared each other's burdens and encouraged one another toward progress, determined that God would work our tragedies into something good. Tears streamed down her face now as she threw her arms around me.

"I knew it!" she said. "I knew it all along! You're going to walk!"

Startled, her words hit me like a freight train, snapping me into the realization of what just happened. I walked! It wasn't how I dreamed it would look, but it was a step...a tiny, wonderful, monumental first step! God *was* faithful. Hugging Virginia's neck, I began to sob.

Just like Virginia, Phil knew deep down this day would come. Many days I wasn't so sure. The constant struggle with my body's weakness wore me down and allowed doubt to seep in. Grief dictated my attitude to the point of eroding my husband's joy, and turning his duties into drudgery. Yet all the while, Phil never let go of hope. With bold determination he continued to pray and expect God to work a miracle, rejoicing with each sign of progress, no matter how insignificant. It was only because of God – and Phil – that I didn't give up. I couldn't bear to disappoint either of them.

As I shared this momentous milestone with my tearful husband, joy, peace, and gratitude flooded me again, and a river of tears cascaded down my face.

"Remember what you said to me when I first learned I was paralyzed? You said, 'You can't feel or move anything right now, but don't worry, you will'..."

Phil nodded, still speechless.

"You were right. You never gave up on God," I said, "and because of that, God has not given up on me."

A single tear let loose and trailed down Phil's cheek.

"I told you so," he teased, finally finding composure. "It's gonna happen, you are going to walk. The step you took today is only the first of more than we can imagine."

Joy Set Free

Let me hear joy and gladness; let the
bones you have crushed rejoice.

PSALMS 51:8

"Pam's doctor has given a new prognosis for her future condition. They expect her to be able to function by herself in her wheelchair within two months with a long-term goal of walking with a brace, cane, or walker. When we consider how much more God has done than the first prognosis of no movement whatsoever, we can't help but get excited about how much more He will do than this one. Keep the prayers coming...they are truly making the difference."

— **PHIL'S E-MAIL UPDATE**

"Don't mess with that!" I shouted.

Phil's hand hovered over the speed control of my new metallic-blue power wheelchair, threatening to repeat a prank he pulled several weeks earlier. Phil smirked as he remembered. He had turned the speed control to high on the model I was testing when I wasn't looking. As I shot down the hallway like a pinball, I bounced from wall to wall. He roared with laughter.

"Don't you dare," I warned.

"Don't worry, I'm just teasing," he said, "Anyway, I'm not very good with drywall."

I had proven to be somewhat of a reckless driver. After only a week, I had already taken out two drawer handles, rammed the open dishwasher door, and shoved a couple of chairs into the wall. Our red metal tool box promised to become part of our décor.

But gradually I got the hang of it and rejoiced as one of the chains holding back my life fell away. My "Mini-Jazzy" was narrower than my manual chair and rotated on a dime, making tight corners and turns finally achievable. Weak muscles and thick carpet no longer held me captive. By simply pressing the power button and wedging the control stick between my thumb and index finger, I was free to tool around from room to room whenever I pleased.

If I had known how much easier life would be with a power chair, I would have abandoned my adamant pride long ago, but I had stubbornly refused to believe I needed one. I fully expected to be walking solo by now. Once I gave in to reality, it took time to convince the insurance company that my upper body strength was still far from propelling my one-hundred-forty-pound mass across plush carpet.

I nearly cried as I anticipated tucking the girls into bed for the first time since June. The only question was if Alisha would let me. She still shied away from my approach. I hadn't held my baby girl in four months.

Within minutes of whizzing through the house on my own, Alisha's curiosity got the best of her. My little how-does-this-thing-work chick had to check out all the lights and buttons. Seeing her intrigue, I stopped.

"What do you think, Punkin?"

Alisha crawled into my lap, wanting a ride. "Go!" she said.

I was stunned. I thought my heart would burst! Through the blur of tears, I could see Daddy and Grandma Madalene smiling across the room. I had looked forward to the increased independence of a power wheelchair for weeks, but I hadn't dared dream of this.

Thrilled to oblige Alisha's request, I toured her through the house. Before I knew it, my curly-headed sweetheart was asleep. Her perspiring head hung heavily against my shoulder. My back, shoulders, and neck ached, trying to support her. Madalene noticed my discomfort as I struggled to gently shift her position.

"Do you want me to take her and lay her down?"

"No, let her stay. I'll be okay."

I didn't care how badly my body hurt, my heart hadn't felt that good in a long time. I wanted to soak her in. And I wanted her to hear my heartbeat, feel my embrace, and remember my scent as I surrounded her with all the love I could for as long as possible. I settled in for what turned out to be an agonizing, yet simply glorious, two-hour nap.

Slowly but surely the freedom I longed for was returning, one small piece at a time. Gradual increases in strength and independence and greatly anticipated moments of Alisha's affection – no matter how brief – catapulted my attitude and outlook. The closer we drew to our tenth wedding anniversary, the more eager I was to celebrate.

Phil and I originally planned to revisit our honeymoon spot in Estes Park, Colorado, that week. We made all the arrangements back in January and even booked the same cabin. But when Phil called to check the accommodations, he discovered the resort wasn't wheelchair accessible. None of the cabins were. We were disappointed, but after all we had been through this year, we resolved not to let the occasion pass by uncelebrated. We simply devised an alternate plan closer to home.

It took a lot on Phil's part to plan and prepare, but he packed everything – the commode, shower chair, all the meds, bandages, and catheters. His number one goal was to pamper me in beautiful surroundings that were easy to access. He certainly hit the mark.

Tucked into a blanket of golden fall foliage, the five-star hotel on the Lake of the Ozarks was both gorgeous and accessible. Marble floors, oriental area rugs, and fancy, crystal chandeliers graced wide doorways and open spaces.

"This is absolutely beautiful! It's perfect," I said as Phil wheeled me into our luxurious room.

Rich tapestry curtains accented ivory wainscoted walls topped with ornate crown molding. Cherry tables sported brass lamps, and pin-tucked sheets on the fluffy down king-sized bed felt like silk. The large royal suite provided plenty of room for my wheelchair next to the bed, and the bathroom included a separate vanity tall enough for my chair to slide easily under the counter-top. A perfect make-up spot – one of the reasons my husband chose this room. Phil knew I felt self-conscious in public, so he did everything in his power to provide all the time and amenities I needed to help me feel good about myself. He didn't want anything to get in the way of fun, relaxation, and romance this weekend.

On the evening of our anniversary, Phil helped me with my hair and make-up and dressed me in a classy navy pantsuit for dinner. Still, as I studied myself in the mirror on our way out the door, something was missing.

"What about jewelry?"

Phil leaned over and met my gaze in the mirror, pressing his cheek against mine.

"No jewel could compare or accent your beauty," he said with utmost sincerity. The love in his eyes melted my heart into a little puddle. "You're gorgeous just as you are."

As the elevator doors opened on the first floor, the smile hadn't left my face. Strains of Dixieland trumpets and saxophones wafted through the lobby to greet us. Phil discovered when he made the reservations that this weekend was the resort's annual jazz festival. Ever since, we looked forward to hearing the different bands from all over the country showcase their unique talent and style. Phil wheeled me toward the restaurant where the first had already begun.

The hostess led us to an inconspicuous side table with a fantastic view of the bandstand, yet remote enough to still hold a conversation. Once we were seated and ordered our first course, Phil set a small red velvet box on my plate.

"What's this?"

"Just a little something I picked up," he said, with a mischievous grin of anticipation.

I could already tell from the fine jeweler's insignia this was certainly not little, at least not in price. I was stunned. My practical husband doesn't indulge in expensive jewelry, and that is fine with me. I love costume jewelry, and my husband appreciates my frugality. So whatever lay in this little red box was by far the most special gift in the whole world – and undoubtedly the most beautiful. I was right. I gasped as Phil opened the box to reveal a 14K gold diamond heart necklace with matching earrings.

"When did you have time to do this?" I asked, tears stinging my eyes.

"I have connections," he said mysteriously. "Do you like it?"

"Of course, who wouldn't? They are absolutely gorgeous! But I didn't get you anything!"

"It doesn't matter," Phil said and quickly brushed off my worry. "You are my gift."

Phil stood and fastened the necklace around my neck. "I was telling the truth earlier," he said. "Diamonds could never match your beauty, but I wanted to get you something that symbolizes my love for you and the blessing you are in my life."

Phil kneeled on one knee beside me and leaned in for a kiss, stopping short only to whisper, "I love you," before pressing his lips to mine.

Our observant waitress watched the poignant moment from a distance. She discreetly spread the word to the rest of the serving staff, and for the rest of the night, they spoiled us above and beyond the call of duty. Much to my embarrassment, our waitress even announced our special day to the entire restaurant. But I quickly forgave her when the richest cheesecake I ever tasted, lavish with a trail of raspberry sauce strewn across the plate in geometric patterns, arrived for each of us – free of charge. I felt like a queen.

Colorado's Estes Park couldn't have topped our perfect weekend in the Missouri Ozarks. Phil indulged my every whim. We investigated every nook and cranny we could reach of the resort – inside and out. He even took me shopping – a sure sign of true love! Phil wheeled me all over the outdoor outlet mall, in and out of whatever store struck my fancy. I bought him books-on-tape and he picked out a couple of cute cardigans for me, remembering how I complained about the frigid temperatures in the therapy gym.

But the best part of the entire weekend was sharing uninterrupted days with no obligations, just an abundance of time to listen, share, and be together.

On the drive home, Phil and I decided it was time to go it alone with Kayla and Alisha at home. We and the girls needed as much normalcy as possible. Madalene's constant presence, as appreciated as it was, was one more reminder for all of us of the tragedy that changed our lives. And Madalene deserved to have her freedom back, to relish the joys of grandmotherhood, not to mention sleep in her own bed.

The emotional transition was difficult at first. After living together for nearly five months, Grandma and the girls had a strong, special bond beyond the usual grandchild/grandparent relationship. The girls had come to rely on her loving care round the clock, and she, in turn, on their daily hugs and kisses.

Phil and I also heavily depended on her. Whether she watched the girls, cooked dinner, or washed my hair in the bathroom sink, Madalene was a Godsend, eagerly meeting whatever need arose without request twenty-four hours a day.

Still, I needed to be Mommy, and with Alisha's recent change in attitude, that door was finally open. Likewise, Phil needed his freedom and space like every grown man. Madalene wasn't far away; she lived close. It wasn't easy, but with careful planning and teamwork, we all made it. And several times a week Grandma returned to help out and spread her love around.

I seemed to learn something new every day about the multi-faceted jewel of freedom. Each sparkling shade that surfaced revealed the glory of its value in my life.

One evening that week after Madalene went home, I arrived home from therapy to a little surprise. Our new, carefully-chosen Ford conversion van sat parked in the driveway. The funds to purchase it had no doubt come through God's provision. An incredibly generous donation was the exact amount our insurance settlement lacked to replace our wrecked van with a model suited for a wheelchair lift. It even came with free installation.

I should have been excited to see the beautiful shiny white van ready and waiting. But I wasn't. I was grateful, yet the thought of being hauled around like cargo in the back of that thing was depressing. My place was up front next to my husband.

Phil met me in the driveway. I could tell he hoped I shared his anticipation. I tried to fake it.

"Want to go for a ride?" he said.

"How? My lift isn't installed yet."

"You can stand. You've done it in therapy."

"We don't have parallel bars here!"

"So?" Phil said. "I can lift you. I've done it before. I'll help push you up into the seat."

I shot him my best I-don't-think-so look.

"C'mon! I won't let you fall. I've never dropped you before."

"But…"

"No buts! Not that I don't like your butt. Although I've seen a little more of it than I'd prefer…" Phil paused, checking to see if I found his comical interlude as funny as he did. I smiled, and Phil got serious. "Do you really want that lift?"

My husband knew exactly how to motivate me. He knew I hated the thought of sitting alone in the back, hauled around like livestock. I nearly mooed just thinking about it. I longed to sit beside Phil in the front seat, and I loved that he yearned to have me there, too.

"Alright," I said, shoving fear aside, "let's go!"

I wrapped my arms around Phil's shoulders as he lifted me from my wheelchair. I enjoyed every second of our embrace while Phil backed me into the open door of the van, resting for a moment against the passenger seat.

"Now, brace yourself by putting your right hand on the seat and the other right here on the armrest of the door," he said. "Then I'll let go and lift you by the legs into the seat."

"Wait! I don't know if my left leg will hold me up! My right one isn't braced!"

"You'll be fine. If you can walk the length of the parallel bars at the gym, you can do this. I *promise*, I won't let you fall."

"But…"

"What did I say about your butt?"

"Okay, okay, okay... ," I conceded. "Worst case scenario – we both fall, and I land on top of you in the driveway. Come to think of it, that wouldn't be so bad."

"Hmmm..." Phil said playfully and then quickly kissed me. "Okay, focus now, focus!"

Phil wrapped his arms around my legs, and after several clumsy attempts, he lifted and I slid myself back onto the smooth gray seat.

"Woohoo! Look at me! Back where I belong, ready to navigate!"

New carpet and fresh leather never smelled so good. I had forgotten how bright and unsullied everything looked from the front seat.

"This feels *so* good. Let's go somewhere, I don't care where, just around the block maybe, or to the post office. What about dinner? Let's go out!"

The girls cheered from the backseat. Phil laughed. "If you hush long enough, and fasten your seatbelt, we'll go!"

As Phil walked around to the driver's seat, I fastened my seatbelt and slid my palm through the door handle and pulled it shut.

"Woohoo!" I shouted again amidst a chorus of Kayla and Alisha's laughter.

They probably thought Mommy was a goof, but both of them joined in, hooping and hollering at the top of their little lungs, loud enough to make the neighbors' dogs howl. We didn't care. We lifted our voices to the heavens, hoping the whole neighborhood heard us rejoice.

Small blessings sometimes reap incredible rewards. I no longer took anything for granted. Little things like a new power chair, a romantic weekend getaway, and access to the front seat spun a hopeful circle where one good thing led to another. Newfound independence resulted in increased functionality. And functionality in any shape or form – no matter how minor or profound – ushered in deep, soul-wringing thanksgiving to the one in the center, granting the blessings...my Savior, Christ Himself.

He was the key that loosed my chains of fear and worry and set my joy free.

Then you will know the truth, and the truth
will set you free. - **JOHN 8:32**

A Season of Pain and Purpose

Your word is a lamp to my feet
and a light for my path.
PSALM 119:105

It came as no surprise when Phil lost the desire to continue our ministry tour on his own. I felt awful that I was indirectly to blame for his waning interest in something he loved. Admittedly, deep down I was glad. I hated when he left – I missed him terribly. And although it was good for Phil to get out of the house, he missed me, too, especially on stage.

Only a handful of concerts remained on the schedule, and we were relieved. Both of us felt selfish and guilty that he wanted to quit, like we were failing God. But the facts couldn't be ignored. Phil simply didn't have the energy. The load was too much.

In an e-mail devotion, Phil compared our struggle to the forty years Moses spent in the desert tending sheep after his exile from Egypt.

> *I'm sure there were many times Moses missed the*
> *comforts of palace living and thought his daily grind*
> *was leading absolutely nowhere. But...God was*
> *working on Moses. He was making him the man*

God wanted to rescue His chosen people…something about his character could only develop in desert school.

I feel like Pam and I are in desert school right now. I believe God has a bigger work for us to do or He wouldn't have taken us away from the good work we were already doing. That means God is using this time to make us into instruments He can use for whatever He has in mind in the future…can I share something with you? I don't like this school very much.[1]

Phil and I depended on God's word to be our GPS through the desert. Yet many days it felt like our souls were stuck in a haze, searching for satellites.

On one such cloudy day, Phil and I tuned in to the Christian radio station during our morning routine, just in time to catch Chuck Swindoll preach out of John 15. *"Jesus said, 'I am the true vine and my father is the gardener. He cuts off every branch in me that bears no fruit, while every branch that does bear fruit, He prunes so that it will be even more fruitful."* (v. 1-2)

Two words jumped out at me – "cut off." We never thought of it quite this way, but "cut off" is exactly how we felt, and frankly, we were confused. Were we *not* bearing fruit? Hundreds of cards and letters told us how our concerts inspired them to either begin a new relationship with Christ through faith, or seek deeper intimacy with their Savior. Others shared stories of how our ministry helped them find peace during indescribably horrible situations. It didn't make sense.

It's remarkable how many people take John 15 with the reference to the matter of evangelism. And evangelism, of course, is super important. Telling people of Jesus Christ, witnessing faithfully, sharing one's faith – that's the natural outflow of the healthy Christian's life. But for the life of me, I cannot find that in John 15. That is not in the light of the idea of fruit. The fruit is the life of Jesus Christ, His character traits. Galatians 5:22-23 would be a good list to think of: love, joy, peace, patience, goodness, gentleness, self-control... Oh, there are no better traits. But you cannot struggle to produce those traits. The only thing you can do as a child of God is depend upon the Lord to produce those things through you. Begin your day and continue your day in absolute conscious dependence on the Lord and He'll bring them to pass.[2]

I felt like an idiot. Never before had I even thought of the Fruit of the Spirit in connection with John 15. *Duh*, I shook my head in disbelief as my soul snapped to full attention, ready for the outpouring of more wisdom.

Now I want to remind you that the Lord never once commands us to bear fruit. He commands us to abide and when we abide, fruit comes...the idea of abiding in Christ is identical to being filled with the Spirit, walking in the power of the Holy Spirit, living the dependent life...it has to do with depending daily, moment by moment, day by day, month by month on the Lord Himself, consciously depending on Him.[3]

Abiding...depending... The preacher's words searched the inner workings of my heart just as anti-virus software scans a computer's hard drive. Unfortunately, a suspicious threat surfaced. If I were to be completely honest with myself, I had to admit I wasn't as good at depending on God as I thought.

I went to church all my life, and ten years earlier, when poor choices as a teenager finally caught up with me, I placed Christ in the driver's seat of my life. Still, I thought I was a pretty good back-seat driver. I wanted to tell the Lord where to go and how to get there. And if the trip didn't fit into my schedule, I didn't really want to go at all.

Before the wreck, acting out my faith had become something I fit into my day and checked off my list – not the picture of abiding dependently in Christ that John 15 describes. Now I was beginning to understand the true joy of fully depending on God, but that still didn't answer my question. *Why* were we cut off? Surely our lives bore some fruit.

As the wise modern-day teacher's exposition continued, the dust clouds of confusion started to clear. A "cut off" branch, as it turned out, refers to a believer who has fallen into a lifestyle dominated by sin, and further research indicates this passage was poorly translated. The Greek word "airo" is more accurately rendered "lift up" when compared with other passages using the same term and when considering how a gardener tends his vineyard. The branch (believer) in the vine that bears no fruit at all is one that has bent to the ground and is stuck in the mud (sin). The gardener doesn't want to cut off the branch – it is too valuable. Instead, he lifts and cleans it off, so it will flourish once again.[4]

> *[God] does something with the branch that doesn't produce, and He does something with the branch that doesn't produce enough. Look at verse 2...when He comes to that branch that's bearing fruit, He prunes it. He prunes it for one purpose, that it may bear more fruit... Some of you are undergoing the knife, the, pruning knife of the Vinedresser.*[5]

That was it! How could we have missed it? Phil and I weren't being cut off, we were being cut *back*. Phil shot me an "Aha!" glance, and tears pooled in my eyes as Swindoll carried on, quoting Merrill Tenney.

> *Viticulture consists mainly of pruning... Live wood must be trimmed back to prevent such heavy growth that the life of the vine goes into the wood,*

rather than into the fruit. The vineyards in the early spring look like a collection of barren, bleeding stumps. In the fall, they are filled with luxuriant, purple grapes. As the farmer wields the pruning knife on his vines, so God cuts dead wood out from among His saints, and often cuts back the living wood so far that His method seems cruel, nevertheless from those who suffer the most there often comes the greatest fruitfulness. That is the way it is with the Father.[6]

Phil and I were amazed at the new beauty and richness of this old familiar text.

Jesus' message in John 15 began to take shape, weaving a spectacular picture of God's love for me. A view I completely missed, until now. This clueless midwestern-city-kid didn't see that what I considered good and beautiful in life hindered the growth of what was truly valuable in me. I was satisfied, but the Gardener wasn't. He saw a magnificent harvest I couldn't imagine.

The razor-sharp edge of the Gardener's shears snipped away at my self-sufficiency and false perceptions of value, and it hurt. Stitches and gashing wounds sliced away self-righteous pride and useless limbs severed comfortable complacency. Phil and I weren't sure how much more pain we could endure.

Trying to survive the pruning process in desert heat with a dehydrated spirit choked us to the core, zapping our interest in doing anything, including ministry. God had to be disappointed, and guilt's heavy load burdened us even more.

You don't naturally produce while you're being pruned, (was Chuck reading our minds?) *but that will come. The Father doesn't expect fruit immediately after pruning, but He expects the heart of His child to be willing to undergo the pruning so that fruit will come.*[7]

185

What a relief! God reached down and took the cumbersome weight we carried, granting us full permission to lay down the ministry and rest. It was okay.

Something our friend, Jamie Jones, said shortly after the accident came to mind. "I don't know what God is doing or why," he said, "but I have a feeling He is going to take you places you never could have gone before."

Jamie had no idea what profound truth he spoke that day. His words always stayed with me, and now I knew why. They were a promise from my Father, the Gardener, that this season of pain carried tremendous purpose...and was temporary. No matter where my physical healing progressed or ended, life would return. Fruit would indeed grace this barren, bleeding stump again. All I had to do was cling to Christ and depend on His strength to pull me through.

Phil and I looked forward to branches that would someday gleam with heavy, rich, nourishing fruit. We anticipated sharing the amazing stories of how the Gardener transformed these green leafy branches into a luxuriant harvest. Until then, we would endure the sting of God's shears. Pain sometimes eliminates what stands in the way of our relationship with God and ripens our love for Him into the sweetest fruit of all.

As one of the "smart kids" in desert school, Phil had a better handle on this timely lesson.

> *I'm sure I could have learned these lessons in a much shorter and less painful way. God obviously didn't think so. I bet Moses had days like this, when memories of easier yesterdays made the dust clouds hiding tomorrow seem even thicker...I tell myself everyday...hang in there, the story's not over yet. [I] may be like Moses, struggling thru the middle years. Only God knows the final chapter, but I do know one thing. He loves happy endings.*[8]

1 Phil Morgan, _The Inspiration Station – Enlightening devotions from Everyday Life_, Moses In The Middle, p. 21, Jubalee Press, copyright 2006.

2 Swindoll, Charles R., _Exalting Christ…The Lamb of God, A Study of John 15-21_, 1-A: Abiding – John 15:1-11, Audio Recording, Insight for Living, copyright 2000.

3 Swindoll, Ibid.

4 Wilkinson, Bruce, _Secrets of the Vine_, p. 33-35, Multnomah Publishers, Inc., copyright 2001.

5 Swindoll, Charles R., _Exalting Christ…The Lamb of God, A Study of John 15-21_, 1-A: Abiding – John 15:1-11, Audio Recording, Insight for Living, copyright 2000.

6 Swindoll, Ibid

7 Swindoll, Ibid.

8 Phil Morgan, _The Inspiration Station – Enlightening devotions from Everyday Life_, Moses In The Middle, p. 21, Jubalee Press, copyright 2006.

chapter twenty-six

His Will, His Way

And we know that in all things God works
for the good of those who love Him, who have
been called according to His purpose.

ROMANS 8:28

Shannon and Amy giggled at my fearful whimpers of reluctance as they helped me stand at the roller walker in front of me.

"It's not funny! This thing has wheels! What if it rolls away and leaves me in a heap on the floor?" I asked, half teasing, half dead serious.

Amy shook her head and rolled her eyes. "You are such a wimp!"

"Yes, I am and proud of it!"

As I playfully held my nose in the air, I lost my balance. Shannon and Amy tightened their grip, rescuing me as they always did.

"Okay, kids, let's get down to business," Shannon warned.

I was two weeks ahead of my scheduled goal to walk the length of the parallel bars without resting. But I didn't think I was ready for this. I took two steps and was exhausted, physically and emotionally. My PT friends were thrilled, fully recognizing the difficulty of adjusting from the fixed stability of parallel bars to a rolling walker on tile floors. Many patients took a lot longer to make the transition, especially if they weren't willing to try. I may have been a big chicken, but I wasn't a quitter.

Each day I made it a little further with my therapists' help. Amy slid my right foot forward and Shannon stood guard to keep me from faltering. My little outbursts of fear continued but quickly turned into bubbly enthusiasm at the promise of more progress.

By Friday I couldn't wait to share the excitement. Madalene joined us for supper, and afterwards, we adjourned to the living room. Shannon hadn't released me to try the walker at home without her supervision, so Phil helped me onto the plush blue cushion of my favorite glider rocking chair where I spilled the news over a steaming cup of French Vanilla coffee.

"All that holds me back is my right leg. It still won't budge."

"Not at all?" Madalene asked.

"No, not really. They detected a trace flutter in my right hip and quad weeks ago, but my leg still won't move. When I try, nothing happens. See?"

As I demonstrated "nothing," my uncooperative leg suddenly kicked straight out. A few drops of coffee sloshed outside my cup. "Oh my gosh!" I shrieked, half stunned by the unexpected movement and half by the faint sting of hot coffee burning my fingers.

"Well, look at that!" Madalene jumped up to take my cup and grab a towel.

"Do it again." Phil said, making sure it wasn't just a muscle spasm.

I relaxed my leg and tried again. Sure enough, it popped out once more.

Monday morning I noticed a pleased, yet unfamiliar glimmer in Shannon's eyes. She sat awestruck when I showed her what I could do.

"So....what do you think?"

"Just before you got here, Amy and I were saying, 'If only your right leg would start working...'"

A month ago Shannon cried with me at my first step – something she expected to happen. But the sparkle in her eyes now revealed this was a development she hoped for, but didn't anticipate.

"God did this," I said after a moment of pondering what to say. "I've said it all along. He's not finished yet."

Shannon was always cautious in discussing faith. She believed in God, but didn't want to set her patients up for disappointment by instilling false hope. She witnessed amazing recoveries, but she also saw devastating cases as well. All along she said it wasn't her place to guarantee anything. All she or the other physical therapists could do was work with whatever mobility came back.

I respected and understood that. Still, I longed for Shannon and all my therapists, who had become friends, to recognize God's hand at work, to see my progress for what it really was – the work of the Great Physician.

As my right leg moved consistently at each try, Shannon seemed to be caught off guard. I studied her response and saw another piece of the confusing, yet amazing puzzle of God's timing snap together. If my right leg had come back weeks ago, if it had followed the normal course of progression, no one would have thought twice about it. But now, all was in place for faith to grow.

Speechless, Shannon grabbed Amy and a walker, and over the next awe-filled hour I advanced my right foot all on my own.

An aggressive regimen of daily weight resistance exercises ensued. Since my lazy limb waited so long to get with the program, it had some serious catching up to do. I looked forward to the added strength, yet I hated the process of achieving it. I didn't feel the same urgency to move the right leg as I originally did the left, and six months of muscle atrophy caused spasticity to set in. Stiff, involuntary muscle spasms were extremely uncomfortable, and made therapy all the more grueling. Still, whatever it took, I resolved to hang in there. God opened a door to healing I wasn't about to squander.

As the holidays approached, my right leg improved. Its strength still lagged far behind my left but provided enough support to drive me further. By early December, I pushed the walker 100 feet in therapy with minimal assistance and started to use a cane – thanks to my husband who creatively invented a strap to hold my hand firmly to the handle. Made from clear plastic tubing, the simplicity of it astounded even my occupational therapist who had all but given up trying to come up with something.

"Just think how surprised Dr. Coufal will be when you see him next month!" she said.

I beamed just thinking about it.

My appointment was January 17th, and I couldn't wait. In my mind, I envisioned myself sauntering gracefully past my doctor who stood with jaw to the floor in utter amazement. Boldly I would brag on God and His power to still heal the lame.

When the day arrived, I wasn't quite the picture of grace or boldness I saw in my mind. My right side was much weaker than my left, and my lazy foot often dropped, causing me to stumble. Since the cane didn't keep me from falling, I chose the added stability of the walker to make the best impression.

Dr. Coufal stood outside of an exam room with his back to me as he scribbled notes on a patient's chart. As Phil positioned my wheelchair at the end of the hall and my walker in front of me, the nurse's eyes widened. I placed my finger to my lips and she winked, recognizing my intention to surprise him.

"Dr. Coufal, your next patient is here to see you...," she announced when I gave her the signal.

A warm smile lit his face as he turned to greet me. Then he saw the walker, and recognition turned to amazement. Just as I imagined, the doctor's jaw dropped as I carefully stood, and slowly walked past him into the exam room.

"You just made my day!" Dr. Coufal said, "No! You just made my six months!"

Actually, it had been seven months since that first night in the ER when the doctor regretfully announced I would never walk again. And now, he sifted through my file, thick with notes, re-checking his original diagnosis in sheer astonishment.

"Pam...I am...amazed," he said.

I wanted to blurt God's goodness right then and there, but

something held me back. It may have been my own fear, but the time didn't "feel" right, so I held my tongue.

Dr. Coufal tested the strength and sensation in my arms and legs expressing surprise throughout the exam. With his arms poised to catch me, he had me stand unassisted with my eyes closed to check my internal perception of balance.

After what seemed like an eternity to me, I felt myself begin to teeter, and instinctively, I grabbed the counter.

Dr. Coufal grasped my arms. "Are you okay?"

I nodded.

"You made it twenty-two seconds, Pam!" he said. "Wow!"

Phil and I expected to hear how "pleased" he was with my progress, or how "fortunate" I was, but the doctor surprised us. He leaned back on the exam table, shaking his head as I sat in a chair across from him.

"This just doesn't happen. I wasn't the only doctor who examined you. You were a *complete* injury. When I saw you kick your left leg last October, it was like seeing someone raised from the dead. And now… This is unbelievable, Pam. Absolutely remarkable!"

Phil and I exchanged glances. Both of us were dying to know the same thing.

"Dr. Coufal…are you a Christian?" I asked.

"Yes, I am!"

Phil and I both sighed with relief.

"Well, then, you know God is at work here?"

His illuminating smile returned. "I certainly can't take the credit!"

Neither could I.

> *God chooses who He uses to do mighty deeds.*
> *The broken and ruined are all that He needs.*
> *It's not by your merit what you do or say.*
> *God chooses who He uses to do His will His way.*[1]

Phil's song played over and over in my memory. I sang those words hundreds of times from stage, but I didn't fully understand them until God changed my platform from a stage to a hospital, from standing on my feet to wheeling around in a wheelchair.

Joy flooded my heart and soul as I realized how God used my accident to teach my therapists and this beloved doctor to never underestimate the power of the Almighty – a lesson I continue to learn every day.

1 "God Chooses Who He Uses" written by Phil Morgan. ©1999 Jammin' Gentile Music, BMI. Used by permission. From the Jubalee Music CD "Phil & Pam Morgan - What Matters Most"

chapter twenty-seven

Even the Simple Things

*...your Father knows what you need
before you ask him.*

MATTHEW 6:8

I absolutely hate New Year's resolutions. Usually I break them by January 2nd. So when our Sunday School leader asked everyone to announce what they resolved to accomplish over the new year, I cringed.

Many wrinkled brows and noses across the room obviously shared my sentiment, though each of my peers thoughtfully found something to say. Some spouted all too familiar goals of losing weight and getting in shape. Others longed to secure that big promotion. Many said they wanted to spend more quality time with their families, and several longed to develop more intimate relationships with Christ.

One by one the domino dialogue clicked its way around the circle to me. Reluctantly, I gave in to the pressure of the classroom chain and honestly voiced my intention.

"My resolution is more of a prayer really," I said. "By year-end I want to walk, and not just with this thing." I pointed to the walker folded beside my chair. "I want to walk without any assistance at all. God brought me this far, and I know He can take me the rest of the way."

As soon as my New Year's desire left my lips, a strange feeling gnawed at my heart. I wasn't sure what it was or why it was there. Perhaps it was my disdain for the popular New Year's tradition scolding me for playing along. Or maybe it was doubt since I was so wobbly with the cane. But then again, I knew God's limitless power by now. The more I tried to figure it out, the more confused I became, so I decided to stay quiet and not share my precious desire with anyone else.

The following day I wheeled into therapy and transferred myself to the mat to wait on Shannon. Within minutes, she finished up with another patient across the gym and approached, holding out her hand. Confused, I placed my hand in hers and shook it.

"Nice to meet you," I said, "but I thought we covered that already."

"No silly. C'mon, stand up. Let's go for a walk."

"Without the cane? You've got to be kidding! Ohhh… I get it. You *are* kidding. You know, that's not very nice."

Shannon chuckled and shook her head. "Do I ever joke about these things? C'mon. It's time."

I was speechless. If I didn't know better, I would have thought someone in my Sunday school class tattled. Obedient and awe-struck, I put my hand in hers.

"Nose over toes. Use your legs, not your arms, and stand up. Only use my hand to steady yourself."

It took several tries for my limbs to figure out how to cooperate and actually achieve what she asked, but eventually I stood, holding only Shannon's hand.

Slowly and carefully, we stepped out.

"Don't lean on me!" Shannon coached, prompting me to shift my weight evenly.

Over the next hour we stopped to rest only briefly in between strolls. When my strength was nearly gone and my legs turned to rubber, Shannon was called away, and Veronica, my fiery PT assistant friend, stepped in to take over.

"You can do this," she said as I begged to quit. "At least make it back to the mat."

"I don't think so," I said.

"Think of your babies. How old are they?"

"Kayla's five, and Alisha's two."

"Then do it for them. Those precious little angels...they need you to make it."

Picturing Kayla and Alisha's sweet faces and wanting desperately to be the mommy they needed, I mustered my strength and walked back to the mat. Once I sat down, Veronica measured the distance.

"Girl, you walked seventy-five feet in one stretch!"

In just three months I progressed from barely taking my first step at the parallel bars to walking around the gym, holding only a therapist's hand.

No one could have been happier for me than Cathie. Her number one goal in occupational therapy – as it was for all my therapists – was to restore my independence, self-esteem, and dignity. As a wife and mother who worked closely with the disabled, Cathie understood the value of what most people take for granted. She never gave up trying to find a way to help me accomplish any task at hand.

Ironically, my hands remained my biggest physical challenge. I had regained some finger movement, but in comparison to my legs, their strength and usefulness lagged far behind. It took creativity and perseverance to compensate for the strength and agility I lacked and adjust to new ways of getting things done. I learned how to crack eggs, make brownies, spread peanut butter and jelly, fold laundry, write grocery lists...

And now, increased stamina enabled me to stand hands-free for longer periods of time, opening a whole new world for me at home. I could load the dishwasher, holding bowls and plates with both hands. I could brew a pot of coffee, do laundry, make the bed... All required adjustments to accommodate my nearly non-existent grip and, of course, frequent rest breaks. It certainly took much more strength, balance, and coordination than I ever could have imagined.

Still, no chore required as much total body coordination as the rudimentary act of using the toilet. Going to the bathroom on my own was something I feared I'd never do again. Losing control of my bladder and colon – along with the use of my hands – frustrated and humiliated me like nothing else. Cathing was still necessary, but the incredible awakening of my body so far gave us all high hopes that bladder function would return.

One morning during OT, the "urge" struck. Cathie knew all too well there wasn't much time. She helped me into the bathroom and held me steady as I fumbled with my jeans. I never realized how much energy and talent it takes to stand in front of the toilet, undo my pants, and pull them down without falling to the floor – all the while trying to keep from wetting myself.

Cathie decided to wait just outside the door to give me a little privacy. "Let me know if you need…" The sound of success interrupted her train of thought. "Did you just go?"

"I think so."

After a second of stunned silence, we both burst into cheers. Everyone in the general vicinity surely thought we were nuts, but then again, people in rehab understood such milestones.

Once our celebration ceased, I felt awkward asking, "Now what? How am I supposed to hold the toilet paper?"

I was amazed, and relieved to figure it out with the help of Cathie's clever counsel from the other side of the door. I had buried humiliation for months, telling myself out of sheer necessity that modesty was overrated. But I'm convinced God never intended some things to be group activities. Going to the bathroom was one of them.

Each advancement generated an addiction for more. God brought healing in incredible strides, but nothing restored the physical strength and ease I once enjoyed. I wanted to do things the way I used to, the way everyone else did. I grew tired of being the center of attention because I was different and visibly struggled with even the simplest of things. I desperately wanted to blend in. I wanted my old self back.

I wanted *complete* healing.

chapter twenty-eight

I Wanted to Hide

...hide me in the shadow of your wings.

PSALM 17:8

"You'll never believe this!" Phil bellowed. "I just got off the phone with Nashville! We're going back into the recording studio."

"You're kidding, when?" I steered around the corner just in time to see Phil bounding up the steps.

"That's the amazing part! The only time they have available is the week of June 4th – the one-year anniversary of our accident! That means the new project will be ready to release in late August. I just reserved the church for August 25th. We're back, Baby!"

If I wasn't already seated in my metallic blue Mini Jazzy, Phil's sudden announcement would surely have knocked me over. We had prayed for Phil's desire to write, minister, and get back on stage to return when the time was right. We had even discussed it off and on. But I hadn't dreamed it would materialize so soon.

The chicken in me feared Phil was jumping the gun. In my mind, I wasn't even close to singing on stage again.

"I can't deny the providential timing, but are you sure we should go back so soon?" I asked. "I mean, standing is hard work all by itself, and walking takes every ounce of strength I possess, not to mention complete concentration. I can't even imagine singing at the same time."

"Well, let's give it a try."

Phil carefully helped me downstairs and guided me to the piano. I stood alongside as he began to play. Taking a deep breath, I thought I would pass out. Pain stabbed through my ribs and shoulder blades as my lungs expanded in my chest. This was going to be harder than I thought. Not only was my diaphragm weak, my back and chest muscles had deteriorated as well.

"Sit…for now," Phil said, recognizing my pain.

"You see?" I said, as I plopped into the office chair Phil retrieved. "How can I sing on stage like this? I can't even warble through the first line of *one song*! How am I going to make it through *an entire concert*?"

"Babe, I know it's hard now. Everything is hard when you first try it. But we still have a few months left. I *know* you can do this, and I *know* the timing is right. I've prayed about it over and over and feel God impressing upon me to move ahead. The date confirms it. I believe it's God's affirmation. Just rest for a few minutes, and we'll try again. Don't worry, we'll take it slow. You *will* be ready."

I wished I shared Phil's confidence. The thought of throwing myself on stage for all to see made me sick to my stomach. And thinking of capturing my image on a CD cover for all eternity was even worse. My shaky self-esteem wasn't sure it could handle more attention, especially now as my already disfigured face took on a new level of repulsion.

A large, ghostly white patch of grafted skin pulled the outside corner of my left eye down, exposing the red, fleshy interior of my lower eyelid. The constant annoyance drove me to continuously push the skin back in place until it became a subconscious habit.

In February, Dr. Cannova implanted a tissue expander (a silicone balloon) in my left cheek, and according to plan, would fill it weekly with saline to gradually stretch my skin. A routine face lift would subsequently replace much of the graft with the extra skin and raise my eyelid back where it belonged.

The doctor cautioned me I would look like a monster over

the next twelve weeks. But at the time, I thought nothing of it. After all, I was a pro at looking hideous, and I looked forward to my new and improved face. I dismissed his warning, completely underestimating the turmoil my strange appearance could evoke.

After surgery, I emerged from the hospital with the balloon in place and my head wrapped mummy-style. As we pulled into the driveway, I saw the girls' faces pressed to Alisha's bedroom window, waiting for our return. As soon as they caught a glimpse of me through the passenger window, they disappeared. Phil pushed my wheelchair inside, and rounding the corner to the stair lift, we beheld both girls at the top of the steps, looking like Swamis. Alisha's head was wrapped in her blanket and Kayla's in a bathroom towel!

My daughters' hysterical attempt to share my burden was priceless, but once the head-wrap was removed and my cheek started to bulge, reactions of others weren't so funny or endearing.

The unusual alteration to my appearance flung me back into that awkward spotlight. Most elderly people stared in silence. A few asked if I had the mumps. Frightened children hid their faces, and others, more daring, pointed and shouted from a distance, "Look at her face, Mommy!"

I wanted to hide. Everyone within earshot instantly snapped their heads my direction as if obligated to the vocal orders of the child-sized commander. I usually smiled, attempting grace in the midst of my contorted features. I tried my best to remember tact is a skill some kids take years to master and likewise forgive to the adults who forgot that lesson. Truthfully, I was mortified.

Will I ever look normal again? I wondered and feared the answer.

Just as my cheek neared its protruding pinnacle, Dr. Cannova discovered my tissue expander had a slow leak. Doc wanted another two to four weeks of stretching to achieve optimum results, but it wasn't to be. My cheek quit growing after only eight weeks. Part of me was ecstatic that this monstrous phase was over. But my domineering insecurity feared what failure would do to my already struggling self-confidence.

We proceeded with the surgery and hoped and prayed for the best. Initially, everything looked great; the doctor replaced a sizable chunk of the graft. But after a few days when the swelling went down, I nearly cried. My lower eyelid still drooped.

Dr. Cannova didn't give up, but his original plan to restore my face back to normal in a year changed. Now the timeline spanned indefinitely.

"You'll be fine," Phil said, sitting at the piano with what I considered naive optimism. "And by the time we head to Nashville, you'll be even more gorgeous than you are now."

"Ha!" I blasted. "Love must be blind!"

Heading back upstairs to the bedroom, I parked in front of the full length mirror. I stood and leaned into my reflection, closely surveying the fine incisions of my surgeon's steady hand, still red and tender.

Tears dangled in my saggy eyelid. I pushed it back in place, and a single drop let loose and trailed down my cheek. Rubbing my finger across the persistent, white patches of disfigured skin, I thought, *the scars will last forever.*

This was not my idea of complete healing.

More Than Skin Deep

*Your beauty…should be that of your inner
self, the unfading beauty of a gentle and quiet
spirit, which is of great worth in God's sight.*

1 PETER 3:4

"Breathe!" Shannon said, placing twenty pounds of weight on my tummy as I lay flat on the mat.

"That's it? You just want me to breathe?"

"Yup!"

"And that's supposed to help me sing better?"

"Pushing your belly against the weight when you take a deep breath and resisting it as you slowly blow it out will strengthen your diaphragm, and *that* will help you sing better. When it gets easier, we'll increase the weight."

Therapy was my security blanket. As long as I was under the supervision of rehabilitation experts, I felt confident everything would eventually be okay.

I was horrified when not long after my face lift, my health insurance company decided I needed no further therapy, stating specifically that I was "functional in the community."

"No way!" I shouted, spewing indignation. "I can't drive or even pick up a can of soup and put it in the grocery cart! And they want to cut me off simply because I can push the walker four hundred feet in a therapy gym? Have they been to Walmart lately? The last time I'd checked, one trip required more than 400 feet of walking and didn't provide benches at every aisle to rest! I can't do these things alone, and that's *not* 'functional!'"

At the time I felt like the whole world was giving up on me. I expected my therapists to be as floored as I and help me fight this decision, but they appeared quite calm about the whole thing.

"Pam, I know this isn't ideal, but you can handle it," Shannon said, soothingly. "You can join the YMCA and work out at the gym as often as you want. You know what to do, and you know how to reach me. If you have any questions, call."

Cathie agreed, "Just working around the house is therapy in itself."

I was shocked. Both insisted I was "ready" to go it alone.

Phil even seemed to go along with the idea. While we discussed our upcoming trip to Nashville, he issued a challenging and frightening mandate that dropped like a bomb.

"Oh, by the way, we're not taking your walker on the plane. You may take your cane if you'd like, but not the walker.

"You've got to be kidding," I said in disbelief. "I'm not stable enough..."

"You don't need it," he interrupted. "I'll be with you. Besides, look how far you've come. You haven't used the wheelchair around the house for a couple of weeks. It's sitting in the dining room with a plant on it. And you've been walking around the house without anything to help you."

"But that's at home, where I'm comfortable hobbling around on my own," I protested. "I know the distance between every wall and counter top, but when we go out, I still drag the walker or wheelchair along. Outside are wide open spaces. There's nothing to grab when I need help and not many places to sit and rest. And uneven ground presents plenty of opportunities to fall and break my neck *again*."

Phil didn't budge.

"Like I said, I'll be with you – the cane on one side, me on the other. In the airport, we'll borrow a wheelchair to get you to the rental car. I'll just pile the luggage on your lap."

Phil could see I wasn't convinced.

"C'mon...don't you trust me?"

Of course, I trusted him. But he didn't know what it felt like to be me. Not really. No one did. What they saw on the outside masqueraded the insecurity I felt on the inside.

"Oh...alright," I said, giving in. If I wasn't willing to try, I would let Phil down. And disappointing my beloved husband would grieve me most of all.

I continued to pray and believe God could fulfill my desires, but I started to wonder if I hadn't misunderstood His intentions. My legs still felt like lead and tingled constantly like they were asleep, and my hands left me grappling for strength that lay just beyond my reach.

Ten months since the accident, spring was in full bloom. April's new growth sprouted through the earth's warming soil so quickly you could almost watch it unfold. On the contrary, my blossoming return to life slowed substantially since the first of the year. While the world's buds opened wide, full of color, I remained half-closed with a faded spirit, the healing of my face and body not at all what I anticipated.

Cathie offered some parting assistance by recommending I see a specialist about my hands. Scar tissue adhesions in the back of my hands had stiffened my tendons and exacerbated my weakness, making it extremely difficult to curl my fingers or make a fist. I took Cathie's suggestion, and the specialist prescribed several sessions with Sarah, an intensive hand therapist.

At the beginning of each one-hour visit, Sarah slowly and relentlessly stretched my taut fingers for fifteen torturous minutes. I gritted my teeth and held back the screams, determined to endure. It was the only way to loosen them enough to begin building strength, the very thing I longed for.

At the end of our first session together, Sarah asked me to list some practical goals – jobs or chores I couldn't do, but wanted to accomplish. So many floated around in my mind, but one especially aggravating thing stood out.

"I want to use Spray 'n Wash® with one hand!" I announced emphatically.

It may have sounded silly, but clean laundry is my thing – treating stains a must. And under the circumstances, operating the pump spray bottle of cleaner was awkward and difficult. It took two hands. Sometimes my aim was good, and sometimes I hit everything but the spot, including myself. Many times it slipped from my grip, frustrating me so badly I screamed. Phil began to recognize my shrieks, "It's laundry time again, huh?"

With Sarah's coaching, I was determined to singlehandedly aim and spray my intended target. I worked hard over the next several weeks. I eagerly endured the stretching and persistently did all my exercises, even at home. When all was said and done, I could pick up light objects with my right hand, slightly heavier cans with my left, and I could maneuver small pegs into an itty-bitty hole. Sarah was encouraged by the improvement. But I still couldn't accomplish my goal.

One afternoon Sarah walked me out after our session. "So… how do you feel about your progress?" she asked cheerfully.

I hesitated. "Honestly… I'm discouraged. I'm happy about the progress I've made, don't get me wrong, but it's going so slow. I still struggle with simple things, and I feel like an idiot. I can't even begin to do the things I used to do."

Vain self-sufficiency dug deep into my heart over the years, and I felt the tremors of shaky ground as insecurity rose with a vengeance. My hideous face and embarrassing disability were tolerable while I believed them to be temporary. But after thirty-two years of resting on my own grace and strength, I panicked to think weakness and abnormality might become a permanent part of my life.

Sarah stopped walking and looked me in the eye. "What you've been through is amazing, Pam," she empathized, "and I can't even imagine how difficult it must be. But who cares if you can't use a spray bottle with one hand, or open a jar? Who cares if you need help? Look how far you've come. Look at what you *can* do. Look at who you *are*."

As I pondered Sarah's words, I realized my family and friends didn't care that I was different. And Phil certainly didn't mind. On the contrary, they cared about *me* and were more than happy to help with whatever I needed.

That was a turning point for my stubborn heart. I thought back to my New Year's Resolution, and the same uneasiness I felt after uttering it returned. I still believed God could heal every piece of my brokenness completely. I had no doubt He brought me this far. But what I had failed to see was that I impatiently sought my definition of complete healing because I looked through the world's eyes and judged myself by its standards.

Before me lay a fork in my path, and it was time to decide which direction I would go. If God chose to leave me scarred and gimpy, what would I do? Would I love and trust Him, even if I didn't get any better? Or would I turn away and worry, allowing the world's view to blind my spirit and stifle my confidence in who God made me to be?

It became blatantly apparent that a gentle and quiet spirit, as referred to in 1 Peter 3:4, is *not* one of my instinctive character traits. Gentleness is "an inwrought grace of the soul, expressed primarily toward God...(it) is that attitude of spirit by which we accept God's dealings with us as good, and do not dispute or resist...it is a condition of mind and heart which demonstrates gentleness, not in weakness, but in power."[1] Such a spirit could only be developed supernaturally.

Little did I know that through my external weakness God was desperately trying to give me unshakeable internal strength. Time and time again since the wreck, He tried to teach me that my appearance did not define my worth. Just as I would grasp the truth that beauty comes from within, my worldly perspective let it slide through my fingers like sand. I'd embrace the age-old lie, believing that my own standards of complete healing, which included great looks and a perfect gait, were necessary for me to be worth anything.

I finally accepted that God doesn't care about what I can or can't do. He doesn't look at my appearance or my ability. His only concern is my availability to let Him work through me *just as I am, right where I am.*

At that moment I made my choice. I cried all the way home as I promised to love my Lord with every fiber of my being, regardless of what He had in mind for my life. I refused to let my clouded vision silence my witness and separate me from the Lover of My Soul. I changed my view of complete healing and vowed to praise Him every day for the goodness He has produced, knowing in my heart that the Almighty considers me far more valuable now than the world ever did before. In His eyes, my beauty is much more than skin deep.

Sometimes I feel alone, abandoned, and afraid.
The whole world is staring, so I try to hide my face.
Pictures in magazines and faces on TV,
All screaming out the message of what they think I ought to be.
But I hear one voice rise above the rest, as tenderly He says,

"You are beautiful, you are lovely.
You are special and amazing.
You are beautiful. You take my breath away
And captivate my soul. You are beautiful."

I long to be loved, accepted as I am.
It's scary to be different, why can't I blend in?
What would they think of me, if they only knew,
The mess I am deep inside, and the struggles I go through?
But I hear one voice, stirring in my soul,
He says, "Child, I love you so."

"You are beautiful, you are lovely.
You are special and amazing.
You are beautiful. You take my breath away
And captivate my soul. You are beautiful."

I cry out, "God, how could you understand?"
He says, "My child, I know you. I formed you with my hands."

"You are beautiful, you are lovely.
You are special and amazing.
You are beautiful. You take my breath away
And captivate my soul. You are beautiful. You are beautiful." [2]

1 *Zodhiates, Th.D., Spiros. Hebrew-Greek Key Word Study Bible (NIV), p. 1665, AMG Publishers, Chattanooga, TN, copyright 1996.*

2 *"Beautiful" written by Phil Morgan and Leslie Asher. ©2008 Jammin' Gentile Music, BMI. Used by permission. From the Jubalee Music CD "Phil & Pam Morgan - You Move Me"*

Running to Win

*Therefore, since we are surrounded by
such a great cloud of witnesses, let us throw
off everything that hinders and the sin that
so easily entangles, and let us run with
perseverance the race marked out for us.*

HEBREWS 12:1

I lugged a load of laundry into the bedroom, and my legs and back screamed for rest. Dropping the wicker basket of clean clothes onto the bed, I plopped down beside it.

Two black trash bags sat in the corner of the bedroom, still bulging with cards, letters, and e-mails Phil read to me during those long months of lying still. He saved every one. When depression and discouragement suffocated my soul, it helped to remember how many were praying for me.

Now, fifteen months later, a sense of normalcy had returned. Signs of my immobility dotted my world as constant reminders of the miraculous distance I traveled from death back to life. My wheelchair sat silent in the dining room, cradling a gorgeous oversized peace lily that obviously preferred its new home much more than I ever did. My walker rested in the closet, folded and quiet against the back wall. And since July 4, 2001, *my* Independence Day, the cane lay motionless in my car's trunk, only to be leaned upon on tired or windy days when I was out and about.

I picked through the nearest bag of letters. I hoped to gradually filter through each beautiful and encouraging sentiment again. Phil must have read many while I was heavily drugged as it seemed I'd never heard them.

On top of the pile, I noticed one from my dear friend, Cindy Moses, and promptly snatched it to read first. A few lines in, I thought surely this was recent. Phil must have forgotten to mention it. Her words read like a detailed summary of my past year:

> *Last weekend I participated in a Corporate Challenge 5K event – a 3.1 mile run…a killer. I pushed myself so hard I had thoughts of quitting or slowing down to catch my breath. But I thought of Pam, and a story came to me.*
>
> *Pam's Marathon*
> *The marathon is one of the most grueling races for a runner. It takes an average of three to five hours to cover the 26.2 mile course. Proper training is absolutely essential. Endurance, perseverance, and self-confidence are key for successful completion – an accomplishment producing pride unable to describe in words. As I see it, Pam has entered her Marathon.*
> *Every runner must start training for the tough race by establishing a strong base. Pam's training started as a child in the church and continued through her adult life. Each Bible study, Sunday school class, and music presentation provided important instruction. Her training intensified as she and Phil entered the gospel music ministry. Denise's and Jason's deaths served as some of the toughest hills she would endure, and yet they were essential to prepare her for the race God had in store.*
> *The starting gun went off when the accident occurred. The first several miles of a marathon are confusing, and it takes a while to establish a pace amongst all the other runners pushing and shoving.*

*Just as such, the first several days following the
accident were confusing and busy, with surgery after
surgery. But now, three weeks following the accident,
a pace has been established.*

Tears stung my bloodshot eyes as I looked at the date I neglected
at the top of the page – *June 29, 2000.* My heart raced as I continued
to read.

*Now is the time when it begins to set in that the
finish line is so far away. You know it is there – it is
your goal. You can't see it, but you know each and
every step you take draws you closer. Many runners
need someone to keep them on pace with support and
encouragement throughout the miles. Phil will help
keep Pam on pace.*

*Many aid stations along the route provide the
necessary replenishing your body needs to continue.
Many spectators also cheer you on, rejuvenating
your soul. For Pam, many friends, family, doctors,
prayers, cards, love, and assistance given will keep
her striving toward the finish line. Spectators and
aid stations are crucial. Without them it is a long
and lonely road. Each one serves as a reminder of
the goal, and if you just keep enduring, you will
eventually get there.*

*Runners commonly experience what is known as
"hitting the wall" about mile twenty. They feel there
is no possible way to continue. Their legs are rubber.
Sensing they are going backward instead of forward
from total physical and mental exhaustion, many
runners give up at this point. Only those who have
been properly trained and believe they can finish are
able to "run through the wall". Throughout Pam's
marathon, there may be some times when she "hits
the wall". But there is no one better trained or who*

213

possesses a greater belief in the power of prayer and healing than Pam. With God's help, and Phil as her pace-keeper, she will "run through the wall" as many times as needed.

Soon the end is in sight. You've passed the important mile markers. You actually envision yourself finishing. Pride and excitement start to set in. You round the corner, and there it is…the goal. You hear the spectators cheering you in for the final steps. As you cross the finish line, you have a feeling like no other. You are exhausted and excited, tired and energized. You reached your goal.

Pam's finish line will be at the front of a church. It will be set up with two microphones, a keyboard, and a wonderful sound system. The sunlight through the windows will be her Lord and Savior drawing her closer and closer to the finish line. The cheers of the hundreds of spectators will roar throughout God's house and His entire Kingdom. The audience will hear, "WE ARE PLEASED TO PRESENT PHIL AND PAM MORGAN." Then, with Phil by her side, Pam will walk on stage, and they will sing with inspiration no one can describe. It is then that Pam will cross the finish line…

Very few will know what it was like to run in Pam's shoes. She will have the gift of running beside God, getting to know Him in a way few others do. Those who complete a marathon are stronger because of their experience, and Pam, too, will be stronger because of God's help.

Pam, I will do what I can to be at every aid station and spectator's stand possible. And I will be there at the finish line cheering you on as you walk on that stage. I love you.

Cindy Moses

My dear, sweet friend followed through with her pledge. Cindy was indeed at every aid station. She eagerly organized a team at church to provide meals after the accident for as long as we needed. She took the girls to Vacation Bible School and on play dates with her daughter at least once a week. I felt my Lord's embrace through Cindy's love and friendship ever since we met in a newly married Sunday school class ten years earlier, and especially through her support over the past year. But hearing my Lord's voice *now* through her powerful words – just one week before our come-back concert – blew my mind! I couldn't believe it. How incredible! Cindy's letter wasn't history. It was prophecy!

Mascara stained my cheeks as I buried my face in my hands and tears turned to sobs. I sat there with a pile of unfolded laundry at my side and my body exhausted by the simplest of tasks. With the letter draped across my lap, I dreamed of that finish line ahead. It was so close I could almost see it. Family and friends, doctors and nurses, therapists, neighbors, and even strangers flanked the path that led past the ribbon of victory to a road of unimaginable reward. And standing directly ahead was my Jesus, cheering me on with His arms open wide to carry me beyond.

Sometimes the pace is hard to take
The hills are so steep and this old body aches.
Just when I think that I can't go on,
I hear Jesus say, "Child, you're almost home."

I'll run with conviction, determined to see
My Lord at the finish with His arms stretched to me.
I may stumble and fall, but I'll get up again,
'Cause this race that I'm running, I'm running to win.[1]

---

1 *"Running To Win" written by Phil Morgan. ©2001 Jammin' Gentile Music, BMI. Used by permission. From the Jubalee Music CD "Phil & Pam Morgan - Living Proof"*

I Stand

Those who sow in tears
will reap with songs of joy.
PSALMS 126:5

"Look at you!" Mom marveled. "No one would ever know what you've been through this past year."

Diagnosed as a permanent quadriplegic only fifteen months before, I now stood on my own in the church foyer, greeting the first guests on the night of our big return to the ministry.

"Oh, how I've looked forward to this night." Mom squeezed my hand and let out a deep breath as she spoke. Behind her eyes were every nightmare and triumph of the past year. She endured them right beside me, empathizing and rejoicing as only a mother can. And her silent clasp told me she would be there still, for as long as she was able.

I wrapped my arms around her and hugged her tightly, just as Phil arrived to guide me away.

"You better go backstage," he warned gently, placing my arm in his. "Don't wear yourself out before we get started."

"Yes, dear," I said and kissed him on the cheek. I hated to miss a second of the action, but I knew he was right.

My back ached, and my legs jittered with fatigue. Once I was alone backstage, mixed butterflies of anticipation and apprehension fluttered in my stomach. I tried to gather them all up and hold them captive, but every few minutes a few nervous flutters escaped. *Maybe it wasn't such a great idea to help out with set-up today. Maybe I shouldn't have stood so long in the foyer.*

I pulled a chair over to the door and quietly gazed outside through a slim rectangular window, searching for distraction. A steady stream of cars filed into the parking lot, and with each one, my strength and excitement returned.

The scene reminded me of the friends, family, and ministry followers who filled the church shortly after the accident to raise money to offset my medical expenses. Phil had kept my attendance a secret until that July night. The crowd gasped as he wheeled me on stage. Instantly they rose to their feet to welcome me with tears and warm applause. I was overwhelmed. Holding a microphone in my feeble grip, I thanked them for their fervent prayers that upheld me during those long, trying weeks since the accident.

"Just keep praying," I told them. "The next time I see you I want to *walk* out on this stage."

Pray they did! And here I was – minutes away from walking across that very stage, thanks to an ever-loving, all-gracious God who heard the pleas of His faithful people.

I glanced at my watch, and my heart skipped a beat as I realized the concert was about to begin. Pressing my eyes shut, I bowed my head and leaned forward to pray, resting my elbows on my knees: *Oh, Father God…words aren't strong enough to express the gratitude in my heart for what You've done! Give me strength and use me as You will…*

The sanctuary door opened slightly, and Cindy Moses snuck through.

"Cindy!" I squealed and stood to hug my friend.

"You look fantastic!" she said.

Dressed in black pants and a fancy royal blue jacket with satin-beaded lapel, I lifted my pant leg and flashed my clunky, black, rubber-soled loafers and black socks.

"Cute shoes and skirts are part of my past," I said, "'but a woman

218

who fears the Lord is to be praised!'[1] That's Proverbs – according to Pam!"

Cindy giggled. "At least you don't have to wear pantyhose!"

"Woohoo! What a relief! Now *there's* a benefit!"

Cindy and I laughed together, and tears pooled in our eyes as the fulfillment of her amazing prophetic letter hung in the air. From the beginning, she looked forward to this night in spite of what the doctors said. My friend determined to cheer me on through the grueling marathon to success, and now I stared at the finish line.

"Well, I better get to my seat. You go, girl!" she said excitedly.

Her eyes glistened, and she hugged me one final time. *Oh, Lord, please don't let me cry now*, I prayed silently, fighting the lump that threatened to close off my throat. I would surely cry many times during the evening, but if I started now, I might as well go home. I might not stop, and I never could sing and cry at the same time.

As Cindy slipped back into the sanctuary, I peeked through the door. A few latecomers struggled to find seats among the jam-packed pews. Ushers set up folding chairs in the back. Our return concert sold out not long after we announced it; we even reserved a second night to accommodate the demand.

Mom and Dad, my sisters, and their families sat about two-thirds of the way back at my request. It was going to be hard enough to keep my emotions in check. I was certain I couldn't bear their teary eyes if they were on the front row. I would surely be reduced to a sniffling puddle, and tonight was too important to allow my blubbering to keep me from sharing this incredible story.

Through a small crack in the door, I was thrilled to see a large part of my medical family scattered throughout the crowd. Doctors, nurses, therapists...even Dr. Coufal, who had since moved his practice to San Diego, flew in upon my invitation. I was incredibly flattered they all cared enough to support me in my greatest milestone yet. God hand-picked them to be a huge part of His work in my life, and the night wouldn't be complete without recognizing His provision and their contribution.

Phil mingled with the guests and slipped in beside me just as the lights dimmed and the crowd hushed. Pastor Steve stepped on stage to welcome everyone and open in prayer.

"Thank you, Father, for your servants, Phil and Pam. Thank you for your healing and faithfulness, especially in the loving and gracious gift of salvation through your Son Jesus Christ. Tonight we give you praise and glory, and we celebrate your power that has been revealed before our very eyes through this couple. We look forward to seeing how you will use their testimony to impact multitudes of others who need to know you. Truly, in *all* things you work for the good of those who love you, those who have been called according to your purpose. We ask your blessing now on Phil and Pam and all of us in the awesome name of our Lord Jesus Christ..."

"Amen" resounded across the sanctuary. On a large overhead screen, footage from the local TV network's recent news coverage recapped the accident and my miraculous road to recovery. Phil held my hand and stroked my arm, and a few more nervous butterflies broke free. I began to tremble.

"You okay?"

"Yeah," I whispered, trying to mask the trepidation. But I couldn't help wondering, *am I really ready?*

"What if I fall?" I said.

"You'll be fine. Go slow and easy. And remember...I'm right behind you."

"What if I cry?"

"God will give you strength."

Like always, Phil was my rock. He squeezed my hand and softly kissed my cheek as the video wound to a close.

"I love you," he whispered in my ear. "You'll do great. I'm right here."

An announcer's voice introduced, "Ladies and gentlemen, I am pleased to present, Phil and Pam Morgan..."

Carefully I stepped onto the platform, and the crowd rose to their feet with a thunderous ovation. My heart nearly burst. Phil followed close behind as I cautiously heeded each step across the platform and prayed for fortitude with each one. Over the applause an oboe faintly piped the tune to "On Christ the Solid Rock I Stand." As I reached center stage, the music swelled, and I raised the microphone to my lips,

I stand by the strength of Jesus;
I walk just holding His hand.
With Him by my side every need is supplied.
By the power of God I stand.

The lyrics Phil wrote now echoed forth, spreading truth, mercy, and grace for all to hear. Adrenaline surged through my veins. A packed house blotted their eyes and hung on every word as I wrestled to keep my pounding heart under control and the lump in my throat at bay.

Instinctively, I turned to Phil, and once again, like thousands of times before, he reflected the love of my Savior. Strength and assurance twinkled in his eyes, reinforcing my determination. With calm courage, I faced the crowd...

I know how it feels to lay by the road
while the rest of the world goes by,
I know how it feels to be helpless and scared,
Left without one ounce of pride.
And I know how it feels when God reaches down
and with His touch lifts my burden away.
I've been down, it's true, but I'm living proof
that God still works today.

Roaring applause erupted once again. I looked into the eyes of the people and wondered how many doubtful, complacent, and suffering people sat before me, needing to know Jesus was alive and real. Indeed, he was all I needed. How many also needed to know that with God they could make it through anything?

Strength bolstered my heart as I slowly walked stage left. *Let these people recognize Your power and grace in their own lives through the ways You've revealed them in mine…*

> *I know what it's like, to cry out in fear,*
> *'O Lord, why this, why me?'*
> *I know what it's like when all I can hear*
> *is the silence of my misery.*
> *And I know what it's like when that whisper breaks thru*
> *and He says, "Child, I've been here all along.*
> *I know now you're weak, but come, lean on me*
> *And with my strength I'll make you strong.*

The music intensified as I reached center stage, and I raised my arms and voice toward heaven, feeling my Lord's strength. I pictured Jesus grasping my hand and extending his other, beckoning everyone to take hold as I sang one final glorifying chorus…

> *I stand by the strength of Jesus;*
> *I walk just holding His hand.*
> *With Him by my side every need is supplied.*
> *By the power of God I stand.*
> *By the power of God I stand.*[2]

Instantly the people jumped to their feet shouting and applauding, their tear-stained faces praising God. Unable to hold back any longer, I wept, humbled to see God working mightily through me. The magnitude of the moment swept me off my feet. Just as I melted into Phil's arms, I felt the loving embrace of my Savior.

Lord, who am I, that You would choose to use me like this? His voice was unmistakable… "Precious one, you are *my child* whom I adore."

---

1 *Proverbs 31:30 (NIV)*
2 *"I Stand" written by Phil Morgan. ©2001 Jammin' Gentile Music, BMI. Used by permission. From the Jubalee Music CD "Phil & Pam Morgan - Living Proof"*

Never Give Up

*What a gift life is to those who stay the
course! You've heard, of course, of Job's staying
power, and you know how God brought it
all together for him at the end. That's because
God cares, cares right down to the last detail.*

JAMES 5:11 (MSG)

While I am walking again, my body still feels years older than
my age most of the time. Additional surgery finally repaired my
sagging eye and fixed the orthopedic issues in my knee, but my
face and body remain scarred, and I continue to fight weakness and
muscle spasms. Yet I am comfortable with my altered appearance.
I wear sleeveless tops and shorts on a hot summer day bearing the
reminders of the pain and fear in my past. I can pass a mirror and
not cringe. Many days, I go without make up, not because I have
to, but because I choose to. It doesn't bother me when a curious
child wants to know, "What happened to your arm?" or "Why do
you walk like that?" I no longer notice if someone stares at me
hobbling into a restaurant. I'm not defeated that I have to bring
my wheelchair to the zoo.

My scars and disability no longer define who I am. They are part
of where I have been. They are medals, and I am honored that God
trusted me with them. Whenever I run my fingers across the taut
discolored patches on my skin, I think of the scarred hands that
spared my life and kept me for this moment in time. I thank God

223

for His perfect plan in my life. Just as He left His only Son's nail scars for a purpose, my scars also serve a purpose.

In John 20, the disciples told Thomas, *"We have seen the Lord!"* But he said to them, "Unless I see the nail marks in his hands and put my finger where the nails were, and put my hand into his side, I will not believe it."

When Christ appeared, He said to Thomas, "Put your finger here; see my hands. Reach out your hand and put it into my side. Stop doubting and believe."

Thomas said to Him, "My Lord and my God!"[1]

My prayer is that others will see Jesus and want to know Him when they hear my story. When they see my scars and watch me struggle, their inherently curious human nature longs to know what happened. Perhaps through the telling time and time again, many will stop doubting and believe Jesus is alive and still working miracles. It has been amazing to watch God open the doors. He has truly taken us places we never could have gone before.

In the spring of 2002, James A. Fussell, a feature writer for *The Kansas City Star*, wrote about our accident and my amazing recovery in a cover story entitled, "Step By Step, A Miracle." His incredible article hit the Associated Press (AP) and captured the attention of the Discovery Health Channel, which produced a seventeen-minute documentary for the *Only a Miracle* show. Oprah used much of the re-enactment footage when she invited me as a guest on her stage in February of 2003. From there, we've appeared on *Montel*, *The 700 Club*, *Life Today* with James and Betty Robison and numerous others, and we've been featured in *Woman's World* and *Evangel* magazines. From the backwoods of Alaska to the shores of the Caribbean, we've personally shared God's goodness. And our music has extended even further to be heard in Europe, South America, and Australia.

During one of our concerts, I noticed a woman sitting with a scowl on her face and her arms folded across her chest. As our music and story unfolded, her entire demeanor changed. The hard, bitter shell she built around her slowly softened and fell away completely. By the end she wept without holding back.

After the concert, she pulled me aside and shared her heartbreaking story. Chilling details of her husband's extreme verbal abuse led to divorce and separation from her children. The saddest part was that her ex was a pastor. She still loved God, but found that she could avoid the pain and tears better if she stayed away from church.

A trusted friend's invitation led her to us that evening. With tears streaming down her face, she wanted to know how I could handle the pain that retelling my tragedy over and over surely induced. Just stepping inside a church brought her agony rushing back all over again.

At first, I blurted, "Practice!" And while in essence that was true, there was much more to it. Gently I shared a memory that I believe served her perfectly.

During every follow-up visit with Dr. Cannova, he checked every wound. I was eager to show him the ones that had finally stopped bleeding and formed scabs. Without any warning, he ripped the scabs away, exposing raw, tender flesh.

In pain I cried out, "What did you do that for? I just got those to stop bleeding, and now they've started all over again."

"I'm sorry," Dr. Cannova said, "but scabs form scars. Tearing them away forces the skin to heal from the inside out, *without* leaving marks behind. And that's what we really want now, isn't it?"

I'll never forget my plastic surgeon's words. They so beautifully described what God wants to do in us. Like this precious lady, we can run away from God and form hard, protective calluses around our hearts, thinking that the absence of pain is equivalent to healing. But in so doing, we deceive ourselves and allow a host of negative attitudes and emotions to hold us captive from the life we truly desire. Only by facing our pain, and trusting God's strength to help us overcome, do we truly find the kind of healing that lets our spirits soar on wings like eagles, run and not grow weary, walk and not be faint.[2]

God has changed my heart. He has pruned me to the core and grown me back into an entirely different woman – one who hopefully resembles more of His Son. Indeed He has healed me from the inside out.

I can't pretend to understand why God does *what* He does *when* He does. I can't begin to know why God heals some while others remain afflicted. All I can do is weep with those who mourn and rejoice with those who triumph – whether through physical healing or in discovering joy is not reserved only for the able-bodied.

With each passing year, I learn to let go of the past and adjust to the present. I see how God has healed me from the inside out and transformed my heart's pain into something worthwhile. Some days my human nature gets the best of me and I struggle with my limitations, but it all goes to prove I am a work in progress. God continues to teach me how to rejoice in spite of my struggle and to know joy because of it.

A reporter once asked, "If given the chance, would you go back and erase the entire experience – the accident, disability, memories, lessons? Would you change everything to have your strong, able body completely restored?"

After a few minutes of thoughtful consideration, I confidently said, "No."

While I pray never to live through such tragedy again, I fully recognize that only through this painful pruning season have I come to know God intimately and love Him deeper than I ever dreamed. I wouldn't trade the relationship I have with Him now for anything.

Someday I will be completely healed. I may not see that day in this lifetime, and I'm okay with that. I look forward to walking through heaven with a perfect new body, hand in hand with Jesus. Until then, I cling to Christ, who lives in me and promises to be with me until the end of the age.

My prayer for you is the same. Struggles in life are inevitable, and through them, may you grow to love and depend on Christ with all your heart, all your soul, all your mind, and all your strength.[3]

Whatever comes, dear heart, stay the course! Never give up hope in what God can do!

1 John 20:25, 27-28 (NIV)   2 Isaiah 40:31 (NIV)   3 Mark 12:30 (NIV)

Now to him who is able to do immeasurably more than all we ask or imagine, according to his power that is at work within us, to him be glory in the church and in Christ Jesus throughout all generations, for ever and ever! Amen.

EPHESIANS 3:20-21

◦৯ t h a n k y o u ৶◦

Acknowledgements

As a child, I thought I might like to write someday. I loved the freedom of spilling my emotions on paper. It helped me to sort through the jumbled mess and find perspective. I have always been fascinated with the power of the written word, but never dreamed I would experience God in such a way to pen a story like this.

Multitudes of people helped make this dream of mine a reality:

Most of all, Brenda – Our lives are so different, and yet our hearts are so much the same. I praise the Lord that your kindred spirit has helped me through this journey. And who else was more fitting than my dear friend who walked every step of it with me? God gave you an overall vision of the completed project, and you got me started. If it weren't for you, it might still be floating around in my mind. Thank you for holding my hand, listening to my heart, crying with me, putting up with my wandering mind, keeping me on track, making sense of my gibberish, and typing away when my disabled fingers let me down. Your grand organization, insightful advice, bold critiques, beautiful word weavings, and endless edits have brought this story to life on the page. Through you, I rediscovered my love of writing. You pulled amazing things from me when I was ready to quit. I admire your talent, yet I especially adore your love for the Lord and others. I have gleaned so much wisdom from your faith. You are a Godsend, my dear, precious friend.

Clint and Jean Shaw – What would Brenda and I have done without your incredible home and hospitality as we wrote together? Thank you for the sandwiches, the beautiful countryside to gaze upon as Brenda tried to focus me, and Clint, for the tours around your flower beds during a much needed break. Because of you, I have a t-shirt that says, "I *am* writing – I only look like I'm staring out the window!"

Jeanette Littleton – Thank you for helping me to understand that it takes time to transition writing about painful life experiences from therapy to ministry.

HACWN (Heart of America Christian Writer's Network) friends – I appreciate your commitment to share Christ through your talents. Thank you for encouraging and advising others like myself through the success God has given you.

Georgia and Madalene – Your keen proofreading eyes were so helpful! Thanks for tediously catching the little mistakes!

Dan Laurine – I'm amazed how you captured my vision for the cover and brought it to life beyond what I imagined. You are truly gifted.

My medical family: Dr. Coufal, Dr. Cannova, Dr. Schnabel, Dr. Patel, Shannon, Cathie, Amy, Sarah, and all the other doctors, nurses, paramedics, EMTs, aids, therapists, and technicians – You skillfully and tenderly administered unparalleled care after my accident. Your commitment to excellence in serving your patients means more than you'll ever know.

Dr. Caffrey, Ce Abbey, Matt Wise, and all my other SCI friends– I am so glad God brought you into my life when He did. Thank you for your life's example which gave me the courage to persevere and continues to inspire me daily. I am honored to call you friends.

The pastors, congregations and everyone who prayed – You have my endless thanks!! Your petitions to the Great Physician on my behalf are the reason I am on my feet once again. I pray you will never ever underestimate what your faithful pleas to the Almighty can do.

Everyone who gave financially – Wow! We never felt the burden of a bill unpaid during my recovery. And as our concert schedule lightened while finishing up this book, you kept our family afloat. Time and time again you exercised your faith with the attitude that no one can outgive God. As long as He leads you to continue, we promise to spread God's amazing love, power, and grace to those who need His encouraging touch. May God doubly bless you!

My Christ United Methodist Church family – A million thanks for all your hard-working support during my recovery. For play-dates with the girls, meals, cards of encouragement, the benefit concert, gifts, and especially the prayers, I consider you saints! You personified Christ to our family in so many ways, and for that you will always be near and dear to my heart.

Barb Underwood – What a blessing you are! We could write a book of all of our escapades on the road! The "little" things you did after the wreck were huge in my heart. You personally took it upon yourself to be my beautician and spent hours with me at the hospital, uplifting my spirits and calming my fears. And back on the road, your help was invaluable. Thanks for scouting out open bathrooms when I didn't think I could make it, and for discreetly helping when I didn't! Your loyal friendship to both Phil and me brought us strength and relief in so many ways!

RELIEF – Alan, Brenda, Jamie, Amy, Dave, Allyson, Joe, and Cindy – The world would be so much better if everyone had friends like you. We've lived through so much together – births, deaths, car accidents, brain tumors, rodeo accidents, heart tremors, changes of jobs, homelessness, kids growing up…the list goes on and on. God truly has brought us together, and in heaven I hope our mansions are next door to each other. Thanks for your love, prayers, and loyal friendship when my world turned upside down. You are faithful friends, and have richly blessed my life.

My sisters, Sherry and Cynthia, and my nieces, Debbie, Lorie, and Dayna – *Thanks for the memories…* Everybody sing now… Okay, enough silliness. I will always remember when you all came to rehab and spent the day with me. Being with you is one of my favorite things in the whole wide world, and gave me such joy in the midst of my pain. You aren't just family, you are my friends. Thanks for enduring the interviews and re-living the nightmare so I could see God's hand. I love you all.

Rick – Thanks so much for using your skill and craftiness to adapt our house for the wheelchair and for the beautiful sliding board. I was the envy of rehab!

Madalene – For holding my children and taking care of them when I couldn't, I am eternally grateful! Thanks for all you've done for our family and all you continue to do. No mother-in-law could be more special or more loved.

Mom and Dad – I'll never be able to thank you enough for your faithfulness to each other and us kids. Our family has always pulled together when tragedy strikes, and that is because of the steadfast love of Christ you have modeled through the years. You taught us how to love each other. Knowing I could depend on your unconditional love during my days in the hospital and rehab carried me through the pain. Oh, and thanks for carting me to rehab day in and day out! I love you!

Kayla and Alisha – You give me such inspiration. Being your mother is the highest honor on earth. I adore you, and am grateful to watch you grow into truly beautiful young ladies who love the Lord. Thanks for your patience and support as I was writing. Your grace and understanding are beyond your years! Anyone for ice cream?

My beloved Phil – I am among the most blessed of women today. You have loved me sacrificially with the love of Christ. Thank you for not letting me give up, for praying and believing when I couldn't, for serving faithfully in every way no matter how disgusting, and for thinking me to be the most beautiful woman in the world through all of it. Bone of my bone, flesh of my flesh, you are my greatest blessing on earth. As long as I live, you will be the man of my dreams.

Finally and most importantly, my God and Savior Jesus Christ– This is Your story, and I thank You for choosing me to deliver it. No amount of thanks could ever be enough for all You've done and all You've given. You've taught me to love You always, and praise You every day, for when everything else fails, and no one understands, You hold me safe within Your embrace. You are my hiding place, You are my refuge, You are my strength... You are my life.

About the Authors

Pam Morgan is a speaker and recording artist who has been featured in metropolitan newspapers across the country and in magazines such as Woman's World, Evangel, and Today's Christian Woman. She has also appeared on various radio and television shows, including *Oprah, Montel, 700 Club, Life Today* with James Robison, and the Discovery Health Channel's *Only A Miracle.* An adaptation of the chapter *Perfect Timing* has been included in <u>God Encounters</u>, a book of short stories compiled by James Stuart Bell and published by Howard Books, a division of Simon & Schuster, Inc.

Pam and her singer/songwriter husband, Phil Morgan, have released nine gospel CDs and travel nationwide, inspiring audiences from Alaska to the Caribbean. Their music has reached around the world to Europe, South America, and Australia and is available on iTunes. In 2007, Phil and Pam were recognized for their support of the Fort Riley Community at the National Prayer Luncheon in Fort Riley, Kansas. Major General Carter F. Ham and Chief of Chaplains, Major General David H. Hicks of the United States Army each presented them with their personal medals for courage and commitment to excellence.

Pam lives with her husband and two daughters in Lee's Summit, Missouri, and enjoys photography, scrapbooking, reading, and French Vanilla coffee. For more information on her music and speaking ministry, or to schedule her for your next women's event, see <u>www.WalkingMiracle.com</u>. To check out Phil and Pam's music, purchase their CDs, and inquire about bringing their ministry to your church, see <u>www.PhilandPamMorgan.com</u>.

Brenda Black is a Christian freelance writer and the owner of a writing and public relations agency, The Word's Out. She is an Agriculture Journalism graduate from the University of Missouri, Columbia with more than 3,000 published works and experiences that range from editing and graphic design to book publishing and oral presentations. She promotes organizations, tells stories, covers the news, and shares her faith through writing and speaking.

Her news and feature articles consistently appear in *The Midwest Cattleman, The Missouri Ruralist* and *Missouri Beef Cattlemen* magazines, as well as community papers throughout the state of Missouri. Brenda's devotional and editorial articles are featured weekly in her columns "The Word's Out" and "Outside the Box." She is a member of the Heart of America Christian Writer's Network and a two-time award winner in the HACWN writer's contest.

In addition to co-authoring I Stand, Brenda is the author of Were You Born in a Barn! Life Lessons from the Barnyard and Beyond, the first in a series of devotional gift books, and Cowboy Pete, a children's story book, co-written with her mother, Jean Shaw, and illustrated by Robert Morris.

Brenda and her pastor husband, Alan, make their home in rural Deepwater, Missouri, serving in ministry to a loving country congregation. They have two talented sons, Austin and Cooper. She volunteers as a 4-H leader and Sunday School teacher and educates her children at home while also serving as the Missouri Cattlewomen's Vice-President. For more information or to contact Brenda, see www.thewordsout-brendablack.com

The story continues on the web...

www.WalkingMiracle.com

Keep up with all the latest from Pam:

✳ *Speaking Schedule* ✳

✳ *Women's Conferences* ✳

✳ *Seminars* ✳

✳ *Book Signings* ✳

✳ *Concert Schedule* ✳

✳ *New Products* ✳

MUSIC Available

Living Proof - 2001

Experience Pam's inspiring return to music ministry with the album recorded exactly one-year after the tragic accident. Includes ten songs all written by Phil including *You're Not Alone, I Want To Know You*, and Pam's testimony song, *I STAND*.

YOU MOVE ME
2008

Phil & Pam's latest CD
with all new original songs
including the debut of
their daughter Kayla
singing *Beautiful.*

GOTTA KEEP WALKIN'
2005

This follow up to LIVING
PROOF takes the story a step
further. Includes the song *My
Greatest Treasure* celebrating
Phil & Pam's marriage.

WHAT MATTERS MOST
1999

Music from Phil & Pam's tour
at the time of the accident.
Includes *Same Old Story, He
Did,* and the charting single
God Chooses Who He Uses.

FROM THE OTHER MORGAN

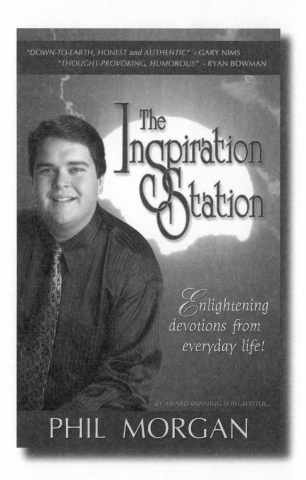

THE INSPIRATION STATION - Devotion Book

Experience Pam's story through the eyes of her husband in this collection of honest and often humorous glimpses of an everyday life lived with God.

"I always look forward to reading Phil's devotional thoughts. His down-to-earth honesty about his struggles and authentic testimony to the hope we have in God through Jesus Christ always encourage me."
- Rev. Gary Nims, Newton, IA

Enjoy the beauty of classic hymns of the faith brought to life by the piano artistry of Phil Morgan. Phil's classical training and creative arranging capture the wide emotional range of these treasured songs, from intimate to majestic.

THIS GIFT I BRING - Piano Hymn CD

How Great Thou Art • *Sweet Hour of Prayer*
Great is Thy Faithfulness • *It is Well With My Soul*
What a Friend We Have in Jesus • *My Jesus I Love Thee*
Leaning on the Everlasting Arms • *To God Be the Glory*
I Need Thee Every Hour • *Tis So Sweet to Trust in Jesus*
For the Beauty of the Earth • *This is My Father's World*
All Creatures of Our God and King • *and more!*